The
Great Dance

The
Great Dance
The Christian Vision Revisited

C. BAXTER KRUGER

REGENT COLLEGE PUBLISHING
Vancouver, British Columbia

This edition published 2005 by Regent College Publishing
5800 University Blvd., Vancouver, B.C. V6T 2E4 Canada
www.regentpublishing.com

Views expressed in works published by Regent College Publishing
are those of the author and do not necessarily represent the official
position of Regent College <www.regent-college.edu>.

Cover Art by Tim Saunders and Jim Chaousis, Adelaide, Australia
Book Layout by Rob Clements

About the Cover: The colours used in the artwork typify the Australian outback. As
monsoon rains flood the land, with rivers breaking their banks and waters flowing
onto parched soil, barren dust is transformed into rich, ochre-red mud, life-sustaining
mud. So the life shared by the Triune God enriches, enlivens and authenticates
humanity. Where the Spirit of the Lord is, there we see "dry bones dancing!"

Library and Archives Canada Cataloguing in Publication Data

Kruger, C. Baxter
The great dance : the Christian vision revisited / C. Baxter Kruger.

Includes bibliographical references.
ISBN 1-57383-345-2

1. Theology, Doctrinal—Popular works. 2. Christian life. I. Title.

BT77.K78 2005   230   C2005-902384-8

To Beth,
in whose eyes I have always
seen the great dance

CONTENTS

FOREWORD

S ome churches are awakening to the reality that they have long-standing members—perhaps even leaders—who have never experienced God to be personally relevant. God has seemed a name to be observed, not a friend to be loved. *The Great Dance* addresses this issue head-on. God is not a "scarecrow in a melon patch." Nor is he like Scrooge, who found it natural to spoil all Christmas festivities. Rather God is, in Baxter Kruger's inimitable joyous presentation, "the God of the great dance." For Dr. Kruger gives us a vision of the Christian life that is powerful, winsome, hospitable, intimate, and oh so relevant and personal to the desires of the human heart with its eternal longings.

What makes this book so exciting and hopeful for the reader is its ring of truth in the author's own transformation of spirit. For it was as a student of theology that the author was confronted personally with the implications of the Trinity, a God infinitely relational, intimately personal, and in Jesus Christ also profoundly human. What we make of the doctrine of the Trinity reveals more of ourselves than what God really is in his ineffable being. So when Immanuel Kant, a philosopher of the Enlightenment, thought the doctrine of the Trinity to be incomprehensible and indeed unnecessary for church life, he set a religious fashion from which we still suffer today. It is as if God is above the radar screen of ordinary human affairs, like a Greek philosophical deity, wholly indifferent to you and me. It is this "eclipse of the Trinity" that this book so strongly rejects. For it has all the makings of a-theism, not so much the denial of divine existence as the irrelevance of God in human affairs.

If, then, the renewal of trinitarian theology is awakening us to the relevance of God in daily life, we are also being awakened to the need to cultivate "emotional intelligence" about ourselves. Joy and sorrow, laughter and anger, friendship and loneliness, are real and expressive of our daily lives. If, however, we are to deepen our self-understanding, enrich trust and faith, make more "sense" of life, and thus cultivate a meaningful existence, we must understand God's involvement in them. As we recognize God in *all* our emotions, *all* our joys and pains, our identity becomes strengthened and secure "in Christ." For we are bound together in the circle of life, as shared eternally by Father, Son and Spirit.

Thus Baxter Kruger re-introduces "theology" in what he calls "the Christian vision revisited." Indeed, we may really question whether "theology" belongs to the academy as traditionally assumed; rather, it is "the way of life" for the Christian. So it is appropriate to use homely language, simple illustrations, personal stories, and lively anecdotes to invite the reader to join and share in "the great dance of life," as it is expressed in the triune God of grace. Yet there is also a place for careful scholarship, wide reading, and most of all deep experiencing of the relational character of God as Father, Son and Holy Spirit. For those of us anticipating a renewed "relational reformation" of Christianity, this book is a delight to read, a challenge to live out, and a clear direction through the messiness of the human condition. It affirms the truth of Christ's promise: "I have come that you might have life, and have it more abundantly."

James M. Houston
Professor of Spiritual Theology
Regent College, Vancouver

PREFACE

There are two things that I have known for as long as I can remember. The first is that there is an invisible river flowing through this phenomenon we call "life." It is a river of glory and abounding fullness, of passion and goodness, beauty and joy. As I have thought about it through the years, I have come to think of the river more as a dance, a great dance, which somehow is shared with us and fills our lives and all things, and at the same time, is constantly distorted. The second thing I have always known is that this great dance is related to God. But for the life of me, I could never understand how this could be so. "God," to me, was an abstract, austere omni-being somewhere up there in heaven, or worse, he was a legalist who cared only about His rules. So the central question of my life has been one about the relationship between God and the great dance. How are they related? What is the connection between God, the great dance and our humanity? In the end, this is a question about human life and the mystery of its intersection with the life of God.

This book is a report of sorts on what I have discovered, and rediscovered. For in my journey, I have revisited the central truths of Christianity—the Trinity and the incarnation—and rediscovered the face and heart of God. The great dance is all about the abounding *life*—the fellowship and togetherness, the love and passion and joy—shared by the Father, Son and Spirit. The incarnation is the staggering act of this God reaching out to share their great dance with us. Our humanity is the theatre in and through which the great dance is played out in our lives, and human history is the harrowing experience through which we are educated as to the truth of our identity.

The first four chapters of this book were originally delivered as lectures at the 2nd Annual Perichoresis Conference, at Coromandel Valley Uniting Church in Adelaide, Australia. I have added a fifth chapter to fill out the picture. I am very grateful to Jim and Linda Chaousis, and Bruce and Sarah Wauchope, for their overflowing hospitality in Adelaide, and for the hours and hours of delightful and stimulating conversation shared with them. But more than this, I am grateful for the light in their eyes and the hunger in their hearts, and for their eagerness to share and learn. Not a little of this book owes much to Jim and Bruce. I should also express my gratitude to Deane Metheringham, pastor of "Coro" Church, for his willingness to give Perichoresis Down Under a place to have its conferences. But to put it this way is almost an insult, as Deane is a man on fire for the truth and its communication. He opened his heart and facility to us with great eagerness, and jump-started our conferences with his passion. Thanks, Deane, for being who you are.

For the past five years I have been the director of Perichoresis, Inc., in Jackson, Mississippi. It is our mission to hammer out a fresh, clear and liveable Christian theology that is faithful to the cardinal doctrines of the Trinity and the incarnation, and is most real and practical and accessible to the average person. I wish to express my admiration for the men and women who form the fellowship of our ministry. Without them and their fellowship and encouragement and commitment, this book, and all the others, would never have been written. It has been a glorious affliction for us all. Thanks for the gift of time and the call to press on that come from your hearts.

No man is an island, and certainly no one has original thoughts, for all thoughts—even God's—arise in fellowship and owe their existence to the camaraderie of others. This book has been brewing for years, and every thought has been borne in the long and wonderful dialog that I have shared with David Upshaw. I owe more than I can say to David, and with David, to Cary Stockett, Mark Simpson, Dan Wills and Clay Alexander, who make up our Thursday discussion group. The insights, the laughter and free-flowing fellowship, the zeal for truth, and, not least the courage of these men to think, has inspired me and demanded my very best.

It is a special gift to have an editor who understands your heart and helps you say what you mean, and does so with grace and style and clarity. Whatever is good about this book, its readability and simplicity, its pace and poetry, is due to the care of Patty Causey. Thanks, Patty, for your time and your heart, for caring as you do, and for your patience and gentle correction.

If you are a man, as Kipling said, when you can keep your head as all about you are losing theirs and blaming it on you, then you are a wife when you are the presence which comforts in the great storms, the wind underneath your husband's wings, and the joy of his heart. To Beth, my wife of 18 years, this book is dedicated in sheer respect and gratitude.

C. Baxter Kruger
Easter, 2000

1

PIERCING THE VEIL

The Trinity and the Logic of the Universe

The whole dance, or drama, or pattern of this three-Personal life is to be played out in each one of us. —C.S. Lewis[1]

One of the great moments of the last century happened when a young boy named C.S. Lewis stood beside a flowering currant bush outside his home in Ireland.[2] As he stood there, Lewis tells us, his mind drifted back a few years to another morning when his brother, Warren, showed him his toy garden. Warren's play garden was not much more than a biscuit tin filled with leaves and sticks and moss, nothing extraordinary. And remembering it, while standing by that bush, was nothing extraordinary. But somehow, in the mix of the moment, something extraordinary did happen. A feeling that Lewis had never known swept through his heart. It was a sensation of the profoundest sort, more of an encounter, and it left him breathless and longing.

Through a memory of an ordinary moment of childhood play, Lewis encountered something that was larger than life, something greater and more beautiful than anything he had ever known. He had no idea what it was, or where it came from, or why it happened, but he knew that it was the best of all things. And he knew that whatever it was, he wanted to drink his fill of it.

At key moments in his early life, Lewis had similar experiences. They were always powerful, but fleeting. And they always stirred an inconsolable longing in the marrow of his soul. Lewis was being wooed by what he eventually came to call "joy." It haunted him, and like Solomon, he turned over every leaf in his universe to find it. As the years rolled by, his quest for joy became the only quest that mattered. In his search, Lewis finally stumbled into God and was summarily shocked to discover that joy and God were connected. He says that he had never had so much as a hint that there was a relationship between God and joy.[3] It had never occurred to him.

"Joy," for Lewis, is not to be equated with "happiness." The difference between the two is akin to that between a five-course meal at a great French restaurant and a piece of chocolate. But having said this, the delight of a great meal doesn't last long either, and "joy" is about both delight and its ever presence—and perhaps even more important, "joy" is about that delight and ever presence filling our lives and all things. What Lewis was after was not a moment or two of a good feeling. He was after a total baptism in beauty and glory and delight, a baptism that would flow over into every nook and cranny of his humanity.

What fascinates me about Lewis is his *shock* at discovering that joy and God go together. Lewis grew up in the Christian West, in Ireland and England. He grew up in the Church, at least until he was old enough to make his own decisions. How can it be that it never crossed his mind that "joy" might be related to God? What has the Western world been told about God such that a man so steeped in its Christian tradition, a man with such intelligence and breadth of reading, a man with the best education that that world has to offer, could be astonished to discover that his quest for *life* was answered in God?

The Western world has come a long way since the days of Martin Luther and the great Reformation. With Luther we have a man utterly riddled with guilt and fear, a man desperately searching for forgiveness—to the point of crawling up steps on his hands and knees in his quest for a gracious God. With Lewis we have a man searching for *life*, not forgiveness. The two are related, of course, but they are distinct. And the difference between searching for forgiveness and the quest for life in all its fullness is the difference between 1500 and 2000 A.D. But that is only one difference. Luther knew that the answer was in God. That fact never crossed Lewis' mind!

Lewis' shock at discovering that the *life* he searched for was connected with God speaks volumes to us—not about Lewis or God *per se*, but about the way God has come to be perceived in the Western world. Lewis' quest, and his surprise, allow us to peer inside the corporate soul of the Western world. For Lewis is not a stranger to us. His journey is not foreign. The same longing for joy that haunted him, haunts us. And the same veil that blinded him, blinds us.

Lewis' surprise is telling us that something has gone horribly wrong, that there has been a fundamental breakdown in our thinking about God. Somewhere along the way we have gotten the "God thing" seriously confused, and that confusion has left us in a very strange predicament. We are in the hunt for life, to be sure, for wholeness and meaning and joy, and we are driven with the same passion as Luther and Lewis, but we are knocking on the wrong doors. Without God we will never find our resolution, and thus the life for which we are searching. But the way He has been portrayed in the Western world keeps us from even suspecting that *God* might be the answer to the passion of our hearts. The quest for life drives us, but we are doomed never to find the answer, and thus doomed to live with a gnawing sense of loss, with anxiety and franticness and quiet desperation, doomed to live in boredom with being alive. For like the early Lewis, we have dismissed the "God thing" as being irrelevant to our longing for life. After all, what has "religion" to do with *life?*

This book grows out of my own quest for life and out of my journey through the confusion back to the real God, and thus out of wrestling with what has happened to our thinking and how we have gotten so far off-track. My aim here is not argument. My aim is to pierce the veil so that we can see the sheer beauty of God, and in such light see what this God has planned for us and accomplished in Jesus Christ. All of this is in the hope that we may see ourselves in an astonishing light, that we may discover our true identity—who we really are—and thus understand what is happening in our lives and how to move forward toward joy.

THE RIDDLE OF MY LIFE

I did not have a powerful revelation of "joy" as Lewis did. As far as I can remember, there were no special encounters or extraordinary moments of insight in my early childhood. For me there was simply an abiding and indisputable awareness that something vast and deep and ancient and beautiful is moving through the scenes of human life. For me it was a given that human beings are part of something magnificent, that there is an invisible river of sorts running through our lives, that we are part of a great dance. I do not know how I came by this knowledge. It was always just *there*. It never occurred to me to question it. To do so would have been a violation of something more real to me than my own existence.

It was also a given that, whatever this river was, this great dance, the passion of my heart was to be in the middle of it. It is hard to imagine a person on the planet who does not want the same thing. In one way or another, aren't we all after the great dance? Is that not the story of our lives, our deepest longing? To my mind, the central passion of the human heart is to be filled with the great dance, and the chief and maddening riddle of human life is to understand what the dance is and how to live in it.

The other part of the equation of my journey is that I grew up in the Church—and when I say "in the church," I mean it. If the doors of the church were opened, my family was there; we were always there—Sunday morning, Sunday night, youth group, Wednesday night prayer meeting. We even went to church when we were on vacation. I think I ended up with something like a 13-year perfect attendance Sunday School pin. To tell you the truth, I really didn't mind all that church. Most young people innately find church boring, but for me, while the service was certainly sterile, the Sunday School classes were stimulating, especially Guy Magee's, which was always filled with history. And the sermons too were almost always engaging. The long and short of it is that the Presbyterian Church of my youth gave me a definite and lasting gift, for which I will always be grateful. It taught me that what I was after was directly related to God.

That fact is beautifully enshrined in the first question and answer of the Shorter Catechism: "What is the chief end of man? Man's chief end is to glorify God, and enjoy him forever."[4] So, unlike Lewis, I knew that what I was searching for was related to God. I knew that the invisible river moving through life, the great dance, was a divine reality. My problem was that I could never connect the dots. I could never see how they were related.

While the Church gave me a head start, it also created a problem that complicated the riddle. The problem was not so much the Church itself, and certainly not the people, as it was the theology it handed on, and specifically its basic vision of God. Here is the definition of God set forward in the Larger Catechism.

> Q. 7. What is God?
> A. God is a Spirit, in and of himself infinite in being, glory, blessedness, and perfection; all-sufficient, eternal, unchangeable, incomprehensible, everywhere present, almighty; knowing all things, most wise, most holy, most just, most merciful and gracious, long-suffering, and abundant in goodness and truth.[5]

It is this God, this severely abstract divinity, that created the dilemma for me. On the one side, I knew about the river, the joy, the great dance. On the other side, I knew that it was related to God. But the bewildering question was, How could this be? How could this abstract divinity, this infinite, distant, austere omni-being, be connected to the great dance in any way at all? This God was certainly in control, absolutely so, down to the last molecule, but this God had no face, no real personality, no *life*. How could "glorifying God" be related to the "enjoyment" of anything? That was the riddle of my youth—and my life.

Two other facts deepened the riddle. The first was the nature of Sunday morning worship. I always assumed that the threshold of the church was charged with some kind of mystical power of transformation, for everyone who crossed it decisively changed. Our personalities were altered. Outside there were smiles and laughter and humanity. But once we crossed the threshold, every one of us went on to religious autopilot. It was very noticeable even to a young boy. The threshold could silence the most boisterous of us and, I suppose, even "wipe the smile off a 'possum."

The second factor came from the highly committed religious types. Naturally I assumed that these types walked more closely with God than the rest of us. They certainly appeared to do so. As far as I could tell, they were good people, and honorable, but they were about as interesting as a fence post. The highly committed religious types always struck me as being a shade or two on the nerdy side and heavy into religion because they could not do anything else. And the force of the threshold was obviously with them. Their presence alone could change people. Their presence could shut down laughter and stifle the best of parties. Whatever the highly committed religious types were, it was very clear to me that they did not have much of that invisible river about them. They certainly knew a lot about the Bible, and they talked frequently about God, but they did not know much about the great dance and how to live in it.

The God of my youth was the supreme, all-powerful being with no face and no personality. With weekly regularity, the threshold confirmed this basic vision of God as we all left our personalities at the door and entered to worship Him. The highly committed religious types confirmed the distance of God from ordinary life and all things human, as well as the suspicion that if God was tuned in to life on earth, it was all about rules and regulations and getting it right. So the great riddle for me was how this God could be related to the great dance of life.

Like Lewis, I could never connect God and joy, God and beauty, God and life. It made no sense to me whatever to talk about enjoying anything and glorifying God. But I knew somehow it had to be so, even though I could not see it. I could not connect the dots. All I could think was, "If you throw your life into 'the God thing,' you will end up missing the glory and the dance altogether." The only way I could see it was that the enjoyment of life, the passion and adventure of living, and everything that makes life good were on one side, and this "God stuff" was on the other. It was an either/or proposition, as far as I could tell. Either God or life, either God or joy, either God or the dance. To put them together made absolutely no sense to me. They were opposite ends of the pole.

Inside of me was a great tension. I was not about to give up on finding the great dance of life. It was too precious, too good, too real. Neither could I give up the idea that it was somehow related to God. It horrified me to think of being a theologian. I was not about to spend my life reading religious insurance manuals, cut off from baseball and laughter and crawfish boils. The only thing worse would be to be a preacher. But I knew that the answer was in God. So I went off to seminary thinking that I would at last sort it all through. I did not go because I was called to preach. I wanted no part of that, and still kick against those goads. I went because I had a knot in my gut and was driven to find resolution. And I got some great pieces to the puzzle in seminary, but not the answer. The connection still eluded me. It still seemed to me that if you do "the God thing," then you give up on life, on the river and the great dance.

The next thing I knew, my wife and I were in Scotland, freezing to death, and I was studying theology under Professor James Torrance at Kings College in Aberdeen. There was more light in his lectures than I imagined possible. In all his lectures he kept coming back to the Father-Son relationship. "The heart of the New Testament," he would say, "is the relationship between the Father and the Son."[6] Again and again he would repeat the point and expand it, helping us see that everything flows out of this central relationship. This emphasis was echoed in the powerful writings of Professor T. F. Torrance, James' older brother, which I was studying daily.

CONNECTING THE DOTS

Under the Torrance brothers and the writings of Athanasius and others, my basic notion of God was being converted. It was moving from the abstract to the concrete, from the austere to the personal. And in the midst of that intellectual transition, something very powerful happened to bring the truth about God home to my heart. It happened on August 16, 1987, 1:07 p.m., Sunday afternoon, Aberdeen Maternity Hospital, Aberdeen, Scotland. It was the greatest moment of my life, to that point—the birth of our firstborn, a son, James Edward Baxter Kruger. It had been a long, long labor (30 hours at least), but now Beth and I held our baby boy and we wept together in the joy of it all. I had never experienced anything like it. The nurses finally pried me away and ran me out so Beth could rest. I drove home from Aberdeen to Banchory the back way through the Scottish hills.

I remember noticing that it was an exceptionally beautiful day, not a cloud in the sky, no rain, no darkness, nothing but pure sunshine, and almost warm. I remember going through a round-about and looking up at the hills and the sunshine, and for a second I swear the whole earth stopped and rejoiced with me. I swear the mountains sang. It was biblical stuff, the trees clapped their hands in joy. I saw the beauty of it all, the glory and the joy and the great dance of life, as I had never seen it before. I experienced it, tasted it, was baptized in it.

And there and then, in that moment, I suddenly realized the problem of my life. All along I had been thinking about God the wrong way. All along I had misjudged the very being of God. I had been a blind idiot. God is not some faceless, all-powerful abstraction. God is Father, Son and Spirit, existing in a passionate and joyous fellowship. The Trinity is not three highly committed religious types sitting around some room in heaven. The Trinity is a circle of shared life, and the life shared is full, not empty, abounding and rich and beautiful, not lonely and sad and boring. The river begins right there, in the fellowship of the Trinity. The great dance is all about the abounding *life* shared by the Father, Son and Spirit.

In an instant, all the dots were connected for me. The logic of the universe fell into place—the logic of creation and of Jesus' coming, the logic of your life and mine, of babies and baseball, of work and fishing, of romance and sex, the logic of woodworking and running a Cash and Carry store, of laughter and fellowship, of human history, of *life:* It all came together. And I saw that it all begins with the Trinity and the great dance of life shared by the Father, Son and Spirit. That is the rhyme and reason and mystery of it all.

The vision was so overwhelming that I almost wrecked the car, and I had to pull over on the side of the road. I tried to write it all down, but it was too much. It was too beautiful, too rich. It was too overwhelming, too clear, too simple. But from that moment on, I became a real theologian, a Christian theologian, a Trinitarian theologian, determined to understand and unpack what I had seen and what I knew to be the heart of everything.

It all boils down to three things: First, there is the Trinity and the great dance of life and glory and joy shared by the Father, Son and Spirit; second, there is the incarnation as the act of the Father, Son and Spirit reaching down, extending the circle, their great dance of life, to us; third, there is our humanity, which is the theatre in which the great dance is played out through the Spirit. *That* is what motherhood and fatherhood are all about. That is what fishing and baseball and playing are all about, and laughter and romance, cookouts and work. They are the very ways the beauty of Father, Son and Spirit, the great dance of the Triune God, the glory, the fellowship, the life are played out in in us.

THE LOGIC OF GOD

God is not like that divine abstraction, that faceless, nameless, austere omni-being of the Catechism. He is not an isolated sovereign, a self-centered king who demands that everything revolve around him and be done for his glory. God is not a legalist, a divine bookkeeper, who watches us like a hawk to see if we keep his little rules, nor is He some boring old religious type, a cosmic killjoy who sits in heaven thinking up ways to stifle everything that is good. On the other hand, neither is God like some goofy Santa Claus who doles out goodies without regard to what we are capable of receiving and enjoying. The truth is, God is a circle of passion and life and fellowship.

The Trinity is the most beautiful doctrine in the Christian faith. But it has been disastrously neglected and forgotten, and when it *is* talked about, the discussion is dominated by those philosophical types who get caught up in the technicalities and miss the main and beautiful point of it all.

What the doctrine of the Trinity is telling us is that God is fundamentally a relational being. When we recite the Nicene Creed or the Apostle's Creed and affirm that Jesus Christ is the eternal

Son of God, we are saying that there has never been a moment in all eternity when God was alone. We are saying that God has always been Father, Son and Spirit. We are saying that there was never a time when the Father was not Father, when the Son and the Spirit were not there and there was just God, so to speak, just some abstract divinity. God has always existed in relationship.

Fellowship, camaraderie, togetherness, communion have always been at the center of the very being of God, and always will be. It is critical that we see this. And it is just as critical that we see that the shared life of Father, Son and Spirit is not one of sorrow and loneliness and emptiness. It is not about isolation or self-centeredness. It is all about fellowship. And fellowship means that God is not a lonely, sad and depressed being. As Father, Son and Spirit, living in fellowship, God is essentially and eternally very happy. The Father, Son and Spirit live in conversation, in a fellowship of free-flowing togetherness and sharing and delight—a great dance of shared life that is full and rich and passionate, creative and good and beautiful.

THE LOGIC OF CREATION

Now, why does this God, this Father, Son and Spirit, create the universe? Why does this Father, Son and Spirit create human beings, you, me, our children? Why does this Father, Son and Spirit create the animals and birds and fish and flowers, and the millions of beautiful things all around us? Why does this God create work and play and relationships, romance and sex, sports and laughter and food? What is the rhyme and reason behind all of these things?

When you start with the Trinity, it is the most obvious thing in the world. This Father, Son and Spirit create to share what they have with us. The goal of the Trinity is inclusion. The purpose of the Father, Son and Spirit in creation is to draw us within the circle of their shared life so that we too can experience it with them.

The early Church understood this, and their understanding is reflected in the opening sentence of the Nicene Creed. "We believe in one God, the Father almighty, maker of heaven and earth." The Creed does not say: We believe in one *God*, maker of heaven and earth." It says, "God, *the Father* almighty, maker of heaven and earth." That is very deliberate on the part of the authors. They were placing creation in the context of the Fatherhood of God, and that means in the context of the relationship of the Father, Son and Spirit. In doing so, they were orienting the thought of the Church. They were saying that if we want to understand who we are and why we are here, then the way to go about that is to begin not with an abstract divinity, but with the relationship of the Father, Son and Spirit. It is this relationship that holds the secret to the "why" of creation, the "why" of your life and mine, the "why" of babies and baseball and all things human. The great dance of life shared by the Father, Son and Spirit is the womb of creation.

When we start with the Trinity, the purpose of God in creation begins to emerge. The very nature of God's existence as Father, Son and Spirit is fellowship and shared life. Every thought of this God— every idea and dream and act—is birthed out of this fellowship and bears its stamp. The idea of creation does not arise in a vacuum of divine boredom or loneliness or sadness. The idea of creation flows out of the glorious life shared by the Father, Son and Spirit. If this God is going to create something, then it is quite "natural," so to speak, to do so for the purpose of sharing life. And that is exactly the point. The Father, Son and Spirit created the human race so that what they have together could be shared with us, so that their great dance of life could be extended to us and played out in our lives

It is no accident that when the apostle Paul was grappling with the eternal purpose of God for humanity, he chose the word "adoption" to describe it.[7] The basic idea of adoption is to include. It means that one who is foreign, outside the family circle, is drawn, in grace and love, within the family circle. And the purpose of that act of adoption is so that the outsider can share in the family's life. The whole mind-boggling act of creation is driven by the desire to share the great dance with us.

Given my encounter with the highly committed religious types, I have made a point of not over-instructing my children in religious matters. But there is one thing that I ask them routinely: "What does Jesus do with the joy that he shares with his Father and Spirit?" I take great delight when our youngest girl, Kathryn, answers that question: "He puts it in our hearts," she says, "so that we can share in it."

That is the logic of creation. First, there is the Trinity and the Triune life, the fellowship and joy and glory of the Father, Son and Spirit, the great dance. Second, this God speaks the universe, the earth and humanity, and all things into existence. And the gracious and astonishing purpose of this creative activity is to extend the dance to us. The Father, Son and Spirit created us so that we could participate in their life together, so that we could share in their knowledge and laughter and fellowship, in their insights and creativity and music, in their joy and intimacy and goodness, so that all of it could be played out in us and in our ordinary lives.

THE LOGIC OF CHRIST'S COMING: THE INCARNATION

If this dream of the Trinity to extend the dance of life to us is going to come to fruition, two things have to happen. The first is creation itself, for if we do not exist, we cannot share in the Trinitarian life. The second is the incarnation, for at least one of the Trinity has to enter into creation and become what we are so their life can be on our level and reach us. The Triune life has to be earthed, so to speak, made human. That is the ultimate driving point of the incarnation. It was to this end that the Son of God became a human being. As St. Irenaeus put it, our blessed Lord Jesus Christ "became what we are in order to bring us to be what he is in himself."[8]

The beloved Son stepped out of eternity into history to be the point of meeting, the point of union, the connection between the Trinity, on the one side, and humanity on the other. The Son became human to be the place where the life of the Trinity intersects with and flows into human existence, and human existence is taken up into the life of the Trinity, now and forever. Jesus came to be the mediator, the one in whom the divine and the human meet and share life.

That is what he did in his incarnate life, death, resurrection and ascension. He forged a connection between the Trinity and us (you and me) and the rest of the human race. He brought about a union between divine and human existence. He opened the great dance and drew us within it.

The death of Christ is understood properly within this overarching purpose of the Trinity to draw us within the circle of their life. If we miss this big picture, then the logic of the death of Christ gets very confused, and a false fear of God descends into the souls of millions. The logic of the incarnation and death of Jesus lies in the determined passion of the Trinity to share their life, their glory, their great dance with us—and not just with us, but with the whole creation. For the dream is for the whole earth to be alive with the glory of God, filled with the great dance of the Father, Son and Spirit.

THE LOGIC OF BABIES AND BASEBALL AND ALL THINGS HUMAN

We live on the other side of the incarnation. The Son of God has already stepped out of eternity into history. He has already become a human being, lived and died, risen again and ascended to the Father. We look back upon this event. So the great question for us is this: Did the purpose of the Trinity find fulfillment in Jesus Christ? Did he accomplish this union, this connection between the divine life and our lives? Did he draw us within the circle of the Trinitarian dance? This question is the watershed question of the new millennium. Did Jesus Christ unite the Trinity with the human race, or not? How you answer this question determines everything else to be said.

The answer of Jesus himself is his cry from the cross: "It is finished."[9] And the fact that it *is* finished can only mean that the human race has been given a staggering gift. The finished work of Jesus means that the abounding philanthropy of the Triune God has already overtaken us and our human existence. Jesus has already united us with the Trinitarian life of God. And that means that our inclusion in the great dance of life shared by the Father, Son and Spirit is not now a goal to be achieved, a dream for us to attain some day later when we finally get our religion right. It means that there is far more going on in our lives right now than we ever dreamed. There is, in truth, nothing ordinary about us or our lives at all.

Jesus Christ was sent to find us and bring us home. And he did just that. He drew us within the circle. From this point on we must learn to think about who we are, not what we can be one day. Here in Jesus Christ we must re-think everything we thought we knew about ourselves and others, for he has done it. He has given us a place in the great dance. This is not something that *we* make true. It *is* the truth.

Jesus is the light of the world. He is the secret, the key which unlocks the mystery of babies and baseball, of fishing and barbecues, of romance and love. He is the light which illuminates the mysteries of our humanity, from cooking supper and managing a hardware store and painting houses to friendship and laughter and music. It is all the way the dance of the Trinity is being played out in us.

When you see the Trinity and the incarnation for what they are, you are poised to see yourself and your life in a new light, the true light. You are poised to see that there is nothing ordinary about you and your life at all. You and your life are the living expression of the glory and joy and beauty and love—the great dance—of the Father, Son and Spirit.

A WORD ON WHY WE JUST DON'T GET IT

Sorting through the whys and the wherefores of how we lost this magnificent vision, and ended up where we are today with such a boring and irrelevant Christianity, is another matter. It is as complicated as sorting through a family argument, and it involves the whole history of the Western world—the history and development of Christian theology, of philosophy and science, the medieval feudalistic system, the Reformation, the Enlightenment, and any number of major cultural influences and historical events. Most of us don't understand our wives or husbands, let alone the big picture of Western history.

But on another level, it is not so complicated. What happened to us, what happened to the Church, is that we lost the meaning of Jesus. In the mix and flow of Western history the incarnation got eclipsed, and Jesus got smaller and smaller and smaller—to the point that the Jesus that we have on our hands today in the Western world is a cosmic lightweight. He can get us into a vague place called heaven when we die, but he is strangely silent about the meaning of human life here and now. The modern Jesus is strangely silent about the meaning of motherhood and fatherhood, about babies and baseball, cookouts and laughter, about romance and creativity, running a hardware store and being a janitor, about fishing and gardening, music and the arts. The modern Jesus can get you forgiven of your sins, keep you out of hell, and get you into heaven, but he does not have much to say to you about the mystery of your life today, about your humanity, your loves and passions and delights and burdens and tears.

I had a carpenter working on my house not long ago. He was a Christian, and I asked him if he ever thought about how Jesus Christ relates to his carpentry. He said, "No, not really. I guess Jesus makes me an honest carpenter." The minute he said that, I thought to myself, Is that it? Is that all we have to say to the carpenters of the world, the engineers, the designers, the artists? Is that all we have to say to the doctors and nurses and teachers of the world, the cooks and fishermen and janitors? Jesus will make you honest? He can save you and get you into heaven when you die, and in the meantime he will make you honest? Is honesty the extent of the relationship between Jesus Christ and human beings? Is the influence of Jesus Christ upon human beings and what they do, day in and day out with their lives, reducible to mere morality? Is that all that we have to say?

The eclipse of the incarnation has meant the downsizing of Jesus Christ. It has reduced him to being little more than a spectator who watches the human race from a distance. And the "spectator Jesus" has left human beings thinking of themselves as "merely human" and thinking of their lives as "ordinary." Carpentry is thus solely a human endeavor, just another Christ-less human activity. The place of Jesus Christ in the whole scheme of things is reduced to promoting honesty among the carpenter's guild.

Sorting through the downsizing of Jesus Christ is where the complication begins. I can tell you that the Calvinist doctrine of double predestination has had an awful lot to do with it. And so has the rise of deism and the mechanistic worldview of Sir Isaac

Newton, and Descartes' dualisms between the body and the soul, and the mind and reality, and the rise of rationalism, and the pride of the Enlightenment. [10] Each in its own way has contributed to the eclipse of the incarnation, the downsizing of Jesus, the reduction of Jesus Christ to being a mere spectator in the universe.

But there is another factor, which is, to me, the deepest. And that is the change in our understanding of what is fundamental about God. The early Church saw that what was fundamental about God was the Trinity. But in the development of Western theology, the holiness of God was substituted for the Trinity as the fundamental truth about God. [11] In truth, it was a false view of the holiness of God that was substituted. For the holiness of God, properly understood, is simply beautiful. If we took the joy and the fullness and the love of the Father, Son and Spirit, their mutual delight and passion, the sheer togetherness of their relationship, its intimacy, harmony and wholeness, and rolled them all into one word, it would be "holiness." The holiness of God is one of the special words we have to describe the wonder and the beauty, the uniqueness and health and rightness of the Trinitarian life. But in the Western tradition, the holiness of God was detached from the Trinity and reconceived within the world of law and order, crime and punishment, blind and cold justice. Reconceived within this stainless steel world of pure law, "holiness" came to mean "legal perfection" or "moral rectitude." This notion of holiness was then taken back into the doctrine of God and substituted for the Trinity as the deepest truth about God—the driving force of divine existence.

When that happened, the whole logic of the universe changed, and with it the logic of creation, the logic of the incarnation and the death of Christ, the logic of human existence and that of the Holy Spirit. It all got twisted, skewed, terribly confused.

The gospel in the Western model begins with the statement that God is holy (holy in the legal sense). The human race fell into sin and is liable to punishment. Jesus Christ, against this backdrop, comes to satisfy the holiness and justice of God. On the cross, the guilt of the human race is placed upon Jesus Christ, and God's punishment for sin is poured out upon him. God's justice is satisfied and we are forgiven—legally clean.

In this typical packaging of the Western gospel, several things have gone disastrously wrong. First, the overall picture has been lost. Gone is the great dance of the Trinity and the astonishing vision of the Father, Son and Spirit reaching out to share their life and glory with us. In its place, we have a divine legalist who is extremely upset over human failure and sin, and we have Jesus coming to rescue us. There is no way to escape the devastating notion implicit here that Jesus comes to rescue us from God. The death of Jesus Christ is now aimed at God rather than at human corruption and alienation. Jesus comes to do something to God, to satisfy his white-gloved legalities, even to change God so that we can be forgiven.

Second, the cross has suddenly replaced *Jesus himself* as the point of eternal significance. In what I was saying before, Jesus is the place where the divine and the human come together. He is the place where they meet and are united. He became human so that he could connect us and thus mediate his divine life to us. Through all eternity that is the way it will work. We will share in the great dance through Jesus. Forever and ever, *he* will be the point of meeting, the union between the life of the Trinity and us. Thus Jesus Christ, not the cross, is and will always be the center of the universe and all things. But now the point has shifted, such that the cross is all-significant. What is critical, on the Western model, is that Jesus suffered the legal punishment that was to fall upon us. Once the suffering is over, Jesus himself ceases to be of any real and practical value. His work is done. He is no longer needed in the legal arrangement between God and humanity. Having fixed the legal problem between God and human beings, he, in essence, bows out and lets them get on with their business. At best, Jesus remains important as the shining religious example for us to follow or as the one who shakes the hyssop branch in heaven on occasion to remind God of his sacrifice. This shift from the centrality of Jesus Christ to the centrality of the cross is the great sin of the Western Church and the greatest of all disasters.

Third, justification is over-emphasized to the point of replacing adoption as the heart of the Christian message. The gospel here is all about being forgiven. It is true, of course, that forgiveness is part of the message, thank God, for we are all in need in forgiveness. But it is not the whole truth. It is not even the main part of the story. Forgiveness serves a higher goal, and that higher goal is our inclusion in the life of the Trinity—that is what God is after in sending Jesus. But on the Western model, the higher goal is virtually forgotten. Justification has so dominated the landscape of Christian thought that adoption has been marginalized. We don't hear much about our adoption at all. We hear a lot about forgiveness, but very little about the staggering reality of our inclusion in Jesus' relationship with his Father in the Spirit.

Fourth, the overemphasis upon justification and the virtual silence on our adoption leave us in the dark about our true identity—and the very secret of our existence. Jesus, according to the Western model, came to fix the legal problem. The focus is upon his suffering on the cross. When people speak of Christ as the Mediator, they mean that he stands between an angry God and sinful people and straightens out the legal mess. Gone is the vision that he is the point of union between divine and human life. Gone is the vision that he is the connection between the Trinity and human existence and that he mediates the Triune life of God to us.

On the Western model, once the sin thing is fixed, Jesus goes back to heaven and becomes a spectator, watching us from a distance. The union, the connection that Jesus forged between the Trinity and human beings, is eclipsed. And the eclipse of that connection between us and the Triune life leaves us with no choice but to see ourselves as "merely human." By default, by what is never seen and never said, we are left to assume that our human existence is just human, secular. There is no Trinity in it, no divine life, no divine dance. It is just human. Our lives and the totality of our human existence fall under the heading of "ordinary." Our motherhood and fatherhood, our love and affection, our work, our carpentry, our play and gardening, our baseball and cookouts and laughter, our friendships and joys, our creativity and romance are left outside the Trinitarian life of God. They are merely human. We never even suspect the truth.

The long and short of it is that we are left clueless about the staggering reality that has overtaken human existence in Jesus Christ. A great veil covers our eyes and we cannot see. We have no idea who we are. In the dark about our true identity, and thus the meaning of our human existence, we have been thrown into a desperate search to find a new one. And that is where we are today: 20 centuries into the Christian era, a profound identity crisis has swelled within our corporate soul and it is driving us crazy. We are, as Chaucer once described it, like a drunk man who knows he has a house, but cannot find his way home.[12] The irony of all ironies is that the Western world is crying out for spiritual meaning and the Church has none to give it. Its Jesus is too small.

The truth is, this world belongs to the Holy Trinity and is permeated by the great dance of life shared by the Father, Son and Spirit. You and your life have been overtaken by the abounding philanthropy of the Triune God. You have been included in the great dance. That is your identity, who you are and what your life is all about. That is what your motherhood and fatherhood are all about. That is what your gardening and your cookouts and your carpentry and work and love and friendships are all about. They are the ways the great dance of the Trinity is being played out in you.

2

THE DANCE EXTENDED

Why Jesus Came and What He Accomplished

*The prime purpose of the incarnation . . . is to lift us
up into a life of communion, of participation in the
very triune life of God.* —James B. Torrance[13]

*For that was the very purpose and end of our Lord's
Incarnation, that He should join what is man by nature
to Him who is by nature God.* —St. Athanasius[14]

John begins his gospel with a clarification of the opening verses of the Bible. Genesis 1:1 says, "In the beginning God created the heavens and the earth." For John that is certainly true, but it is not quite true enough. John sees more clearly than any biblical writer that the God who created in the beginning was not simply "God," not that abstract, austere and faceless omni-being, but the Father, Son and Spirit. And John sees that both creation and the coming of Jesus Christ flow directly out of the Trinitarian life. The reason for creation, the aim and purpose of creation, of your existence and mine, lies in the great dance of life shared by the Father, Son and Spirit. The purpose of this God in creating the world is to extend the great dance to others. That is the logic of the universe—the eternal Word of God.

If this dream of the Father, Son and Spirit is to come to full and abiding fruition, it is necessary that at least one of the Trinity enter into our world and become what we are. For it is only in this way that the Triune life can actually reach *us*. Anything less would leave us with something like a blimp in the sky—close, visible, but ultimately above us, out of our reach. The logic of the coming of Jesus begins with the great dance of life shared by the Father, Son and Spirit and with their astonishing decision and determination to share that dance with us.

To this end, the Son of God stepped out of eternity and became a human being, a baby born of the Virgin Mary. In the greatest of all humility, he entered into our world and became what we are. In the first instance, we must see the coming of the Son of God as the act of the Father, Son and Spirit earthing their fellowship, their great dance of shared life.

THE INCARNATION OF THE TRINITARIAN DANCE

Earlier I wrote of the transition that I went through in my understanding of God. I moved from thinking of God as just God, a sort of naked, abstract omni-power with no real face, to the Christian vision of God as Father, Son and Spirit living in a fellowship of joy and passion and creativity and love. In the same way, we must make a transition in our thinking about the incarnation.

The Church, in its better days, fought tooth and nail to hang onto the incarnation. The early Church understood that everything hinged on it. If Jesus Christ is not fully divine, "God of God" as the creed says, then what he has given to us is less than the fullness and life of God. They understood this, and they fought for the full divinity of Christ. They did the same for his full humanity. For the logic holds true on the other side. If he is God of God, but has not become a real human being, then he may have the divine life, but it does not reach *us*. We are back to the blimp in the sky.

Alongside of these two emphases, there is a third, and it is every bit as critical as the first two. In fact, if you miss the third point, then all this talk of the full divinity and the full humanity of Jesus gets lost in abstractions and never makes any real sense. The incarnation means that God of God became a real human being, bone of our bone and flesh of our flesh. But it was not just any God who became human. It was the *Son* of God. It was not that abstract, faceless omnipower who became human, it was the Father's beloved Son, the one who lives in the fellowship of the Spirit with the Father, the one who knows the Father and loves him and shares the dance of life.

Let me put the point in question form: Did the Son of God give up his Father when he became human? Did he step outside the circle of life he shares with the Father and the Spirit? Did the dance die out at Christmas? Was the fellowship of the Father and Son in the Spirit suddenly broken apart and lost somewhere in the process? Of course not. Above and beyond all things, the incarnation means the coming not merely of God or some kind of generic divine life. The incarnation means the coming of the eternal *trinitarian relationship* of Father, Son and Spirit. In Jesus Christ, not just divine life, but the great dance of the Trinity, the joy and fullness and glory of Father, Son and Spirit, their life and communion and fellowship, entered into our world and set up shop.[15] That is the simple and astonishing truth of it.

In the first instance, the life of Jesus Christ is to be understood as the living out, the enfleshment, not merely of a divine life, but of the Trinitarian life itself inside human existence. What happens in Jesus Christ is that the great dance of the Trinity is earthed and lived out as a divine-human reality.

If you start with a legal holiness as the fundamental truth about God, then, when you come to Jesus, you are in such a hurry to get to the cross to solve the sin problem that you fly past the incarnation. When you start with legal holiness, you have eyes only for the cross, and you never see that in Jesus Christ, nothing less than the eternal trinitarian life of Father, Son and Spirit is being lived out inside human existence. You never really get the staggering meaning of the incarnation. And you never see the equally staggering meaning of the ascension. The cross, on the legal model, looms so large on the horizon that the incarnation, resurrection and ascension of Jesus are overshadowed. Do you know what the ascension means? Have you ever heard a sermon or a series of sermons on the ascension? The ascension means that the incarnation is not over. The ascension means that now and forever the Son continues to live out his sonship as a human being.

When the Son became human, it was not as though he put on a robe which he would take off later. He is now and forever one of us, bone of our bone and flesh of our flesh, man, a human being. As Trevor Hart points out, the incarnation was not a "temporary episode in the life of God,"[16] but a permanent reality for the Trinity. Seated now and forever at the right hand of the Father, inside the circle as a full participant in the dance, is the fully divine Son of God *as man.* The earthing of the Trinitarian life, the enfleshment of the dance of the Trinity, was not a passing phase. What the Son of God became is not over and done with. The incarnation was not a moment in the past. When the Son of God became human, he *became* human and he *will* be human through all eternity. The dance of the Triune life is no longer just a divine dance. It is now and forever a divine-human dance. When the Father calls the Son now, he speaks in a human language, and he will throughout all eternity.

Why? Because behind the universe is not an austere, self-centered, abstract divinity, but the Father, Son and Spirit and their eternal fellowship together. And because this Triune God, in astonishing grace, has determined not to hoard the great dance, but to share it with us. That determination translated into incarnation and ascension, into the living out of that Trinitarian relationship inside human existence, now and forever, so that the dance could actually reach *us.*

THE INCARNATION OF THE DANCE INSIDE THE FALL

But we are only scratching the surface here of the meaning of the incarnation. For this living out of the Trinitarian fellowship inside human existence took place within the circle of our *actual* human existence—inside the fall and corruption of Adam, inside the domination and darkness of evil, and inside the covenant between God and Israel. The incarnation of the Triune fellowship was therefore a bloody event, with pain and tears, loud crying and suffering and death and new birth.

Inside Adam's Skin: The New Man

First and foremost, the incarnation is the Son of God living out his sonship, his fellowship with his Father, as a human being. But John tells us straightaway that this happened not merely inside our human existence, but inside human "flesh."[17] It was not good enough for John to leave us with the truth that "God" created the heavens and the earth. He wanted to make sure that we know that it was the Father, Son and Spirit who acted in creation. In a similar way, it was not good enough for John to leave us with the fact that the Son of God became a human being. He wanted to make sure that we see the full glory of Jesus Christ. He wanted to make sure that we understand the depths of his humility and love. He wanted us to understand the incarnation as atonement. The Son, John tells us, became not merely human, but "flesh." *Flesh*,[18] biblically speaking, is a loaded word. When the Bible speaks of humanity in darkness, in rebellion and corruption and perversion, it uses the word *flesh.*

The Son of God entered into the human equation where we actually are, not back in the Garden before the Fall of Adam, but after the Fall, and thus he entered into the midst of human corruption and disorder, brokenness and disease. He entered into the only human existence available—fallen human existence.

Have you ever thought about that? I was always taught that the human race is corrupt, "totally depraved." That may be too strong a statement or it may not be strong enough. But whatever is to be said about the state of human existence and the depth of its corruption, the staggering truth of the incarnation is that the Son of God entered into it.

T. F. Torrance of Scotland sees the significance of this more than any modern writer I know. He says:

> Perhaps the most fundamental truth which we have to learn in the Christian Church, or rather relearn since we have suppressed it, is

that the Incarnation was the coming of God to save us in the heart of our *fallen* and *depraved* humanity.... That is to say, the Incarnation is to be understood as the coming of God to take upon himself our fallen human nature, our actual human existence laden with sin and guilt, our humanity diseased in mind and soul in its estrangement or alienation from the Creator.[19]

The point here, of course, is not to say that Jesus Christ became sinful or that he was contaminated in some way by the human existence he entered. The point is to say that he truly entered into our actual situation. If he didn't, then we are back to the blimp. For his work would then hover over our heads. It would then have no real bearing upon *us*.

Think of a group of people trapped in a collapsed mine. And suppose that the rescue team only sets up shop on the surface and never actually goes down into the mine. What would be the point? There would be no rescue. The help would not reach the people trapped in the mine. But turn the thought around. Suppose that the rescue team does go down into the mine, but loses contact with the surface crew. In that case they, too, would be lost.

It is necessary that we hold on to both sides of the truth. If Jesus ceases to be himself, the Father's beloved Son who lives in fellowship with the Father in the Spirit, then all is lost, for he has nothing to give us when he comes to us. If, on the other hand, he lives out his sonship with his Father but does not do so inside Adam's skin, then his sonship does not reach us;[20] the dance of life of the Trinity flies over our heads.

Once we see with John and Paul and the early Church that the incarnation was a real incarnation, that the Son of God became flesh without giving up his fellowship with his Father, then we are face to face with a paradox that will allow us to see the truth about the work of Christ. In Jesus Christ, a union is forged between two things that do not go together. On one side, you have the Triune life of God with all of its face-to-face fellowship and purity and fullness and joy and rightness and integrity. On the other side, you have human existence in all of its hiding, brokenness, corruption, disease and perversion. The incarnation means that these two worlds are united.

In Jesus Christ, the joyful fellowship of the Father, Son and Spirit, the wholeness and purity of the Trinity, meets Adam, fearful and ashamed and hiding in the bushes. How is this possible? How can it be that there is a union between the Triune being of God and fallen human being? How is it possible for the peace of God to intersect the disharmony of fallen human existence? How can the dance of the Trinity actually touch and enter into the chaos of human disorder? How can this "most violent of all contradictions," as Edward Irving put it, be possible?[21]

The answer is that it is not possible. Something has to give. Something has to change. There has to be a conversion, a transformation, a fundamental reordering—a real reconciliation. And that is exactly what happened in Jesus' life, death and resurrection. Adam and fallen Adamic human existence got turned around, converted, fundamentally reordered, healed—crucified and born again.

The entrance of the fellowship of the Father, Son and Spirit into our broken and alien condition does not mean the ruin of the Trinity. It does not mean divine contamination or defilement or pollution, or some sort of poisonous infection of the fellowship of the Father, Son and Spirit, any more than Jesus was contaminated or became leprous when he reached out and touched the leper. The entrance of the fellowship of Father, Son and Spirit into the "flesh," into broken human existence, means war!

In Luke 2:52, the Bible says that Jesus *grew* in both wisdom and stature with God and with man. The Greek word translated as "grew" is *prokopto.* It means to go forward, to make progress, to forge ahead. It was used in the ancient world to describe the forging of metal in the hands of a metalsmith.

If you have ever seen a blacksmith hammer out a horseshoe, then you have the picture of *prokopto*. First, the blacksmith builds a red-hot fire. Then he takes an iron rod and shoves it into the center of the coals. When the rod itself glows like an ember, the blacksmith grabs its cooler end with his gloved hand, pulls it from the fire and puts it on an anvil. Within seconds, he summons every ounce of strength in his body and hammers on the rod with astonishing blows. Temporarily spent, he throws the rod into a bucket of cold water to freeze the progress and catch his breath. Within a moment, the rod is back in the fire.

The extremities involved—the sheer heat of the fire, the strength of the man, the astonishing force of the blows, the precision—are shocking. Again and again the cycle is repeated, with only slight progress. At length, through the exhausting repetition of fire and mighty blows, through pain and sweat and blood, the shape of a horseshoe begins to emerge.

That is the best picture of what the incarnation means when we look at in its true context. For that is what happened in Jesus Christ from his birth to his resurrection. The Son of God entered into our broken, fallen, alienated human existence. He took upon himself our fallen flesh.[22] He stood in Adam's shoes, in Israel's shoes, in our shoes, and he steadfastly refused to be Adam. He refused to be Israel. He refused to be what we are.

In our flesh, inside Adam's skin, he beat his way forward by blows. He entered into fallen human existence and he steadfastly refused to be "fallen" in it. Step by step, moment by moment, blow by blow, through fire and trial, through 33 years of blood, sweat and tears, through crucifixion, in the power of the Holy Spirit, he transformed the fallen humanity he assumed from "Adam's sin-gnarled family tree."[23]

That is the atoning work of Jesus Christ. He lived out his sonship inside fallen Adamic existence, and it was a bloody mess. He lived out his sonship through fire and trial and tears,[24] to the point of ultimate self-sacrifice in dying on the cross. The death of Jesus Christ is not punishment from the hands of an angry God; it is the Son's ultimate identification with fallen Adam, and the supreme expression of faithfulness to his own identity as the One who lives in fellowship with the Father in the Spirit. For he truly entered into our brokenness and estrangement and alienation. He bore the violent contradiction in his own being, and he resolved it through fire and trial, by dying to his Adamic flesh, by crucifying it on Calvary. For in no other way could he live out his fellowship with his Father—as the *incarnate* Son—except through putting to death the flesh of Adam.

The death of Jesus Christ is not the end of the relationship between the Father and Son; it is its final triumph. For dying is the incarnate Son's final and decisive refusal to be Adam. As such, it is the radical circumcision of Adamic flesh, the death of the man of sin, the decisive conversion of Adamic existence, and the end and undoing of the Fall in re-creation and resurrection. For what emerges on the other side of the cross is a human being, from the fallen stock of Adam, who is utterly right with God the Father.

Jesus Christ is not a divine wrench which God picked up and used for a while and then put back in the heavenly tool box. Neither is Jesus a mere accountant who balances the legal ledger. Jesus Christ is living atonement. He is man, from the sin-gnarled stock of Adam, right with God the Father. He is Adamic man, at-one with the Father, living in union and communion with the Father, accepted and embraced by the Father and seated at His right hand. What emerges through 33 years of fire and trial and crucifixion is Adamic man sharing fully and completely in the great dance of the Trinity, now and forever. This living union, this relationship between God, on the one side, and humanity on the other, is the atoning work of Christ. This union is salvation; it is real, not theoretical, reconciliation.

Inside the Domain of Evil: Jesus Is Victor

But now we have to look again at the incarnation. We are still only scratching the surface of what the incarnation means. The Son of God came here and lived out his sonship, his fellowship and life, with his Father in the Spirit. And he continues to do so now and forever as the *incarnate* Son. But this happened within a definite context, within the context of the Fall and thus inside fallen Adamic existence. Now we must see that this happened inside the domain of evil.

The incarnation happens inside the circle of the darkness, inside the circle of the lie. The Son of God entered into *our* world, the world where the human race had fallen prey to evil and given itself irretrievably into the hands of the evil one. He became what we are. He stood where we stood, where evil and darkness and corruption had wrapped themselves around our very beings and were threatening our utter destruction.

In Jesus Christ, two things come together that do not go together: the fellowship of the Father, Son and Spirit and our alienated, broken human existence under the domination of the evil one. What happens when the very fellowship and life and glory of the Father, Son and Spirit invade the domain of darkness, set up shop inside enemy territory? What happens when the Son knows his Father in the fellowship of the Spirit as he has always known him, but now from inside Adam's skin, and inside the domain of evil? What happens when the Son walks and lives in the Holy Spirit, as he has always walked and lived, but now walks and lives also as a man in Adam's shoes, under the blinding harassment of the evil one? What happens when inside our darkness and alienation, inside our confusion and the temptations that are common to man, the Son of God steadfastly refuses to be anything other than who he is, the Father's beloved and faithful Son who lives in the fellowship of the Spirit?

What happens when day after day he speaks his great and intolerant "No! I will not. I will not be my own man. I will not forsake my Father. I will not step outside the circle of life that I share with him in the Spirit. I will love my Father with all of my heart, soul, mind and strength!" What happens?

In the truest sense of the phrase, "All hell breaks loose." In an all-out attack, the evil one unleashes everything he has on Jesus Christ. He uses every subtle and heinous and dastardly trick he has. He despises the fellowship of the Father, Son and Spirit; he wants it ripped apart and destroyed, ousted from the planet.

Some people think that Jesus was not tempted like we are, that he had it easy, that he basically showed up as the Son of God and everything was fine. The truth is we will never know the cup that he had to drink. We will never know the pain, the agony that he bore. What we see in Gethsemane[25] when Jesus is on his face, crying profound tears and sweating drops of blood—the grief, the pain, the suffering of bearing up under the weight of it all—what we see in Gethsemane is a picture of what was happening inside of Jesus from the moment of his birth. His whole life was war: pressure, temptations from within and without, constant assaults of doubt and confusion and darkness, incessant innuendos, never-ending shame from the religious types, the weakness and betrayal of his best friends.

The incarnation means that he lived out his sonship inside the domain of evil. From his birth to the cross, it was war;"from the time when he took on the form of a servant, he began to pay the price of liberation," as Calvin put it.[26] The great dance of life shared by the Father, Son and Spirit set up shop inside the domain of darkness, and through fire and trial, blow by blow, for 33 years, it worked its way through the whole camp. The fact that through it all Jesus never once betrayed his Father; the fact that through it all he never once stepped outside the circle of life he shares with his Father in the Spirit; the fact that he bore up under the weight of it all, means that in Jesus Christ a man emerges, from the sin-gnarled stock of Adam, from inside the domain of evil, who is utterly and absolutely victorious over evil.

What could the evil one possibly throw at the resurrected and ascended Son now, that he has not seen and seen through and loved his Father through? The resurrected Jesus Christ is the incarnate Son of God as man, as Adamic man, living beyond the possibility of temptation and darkness and confusion. He is Adamic man living in victory, living in the light, unhindered by the darkness. It is impossible for evil to even get a foothold in the circle of the fellowship of the Spirit shared by the Father and the *incarnate* and *ascended* Son. He lives beyond darkness, in the full light of the dance, now and forever. Jesus is victor.

Inside the Covenant: The New Covenant

But we are still only scratching the surface of the incarnation. There is yet another, a third, context in which we must see the earthing of the Trinitarian fellowship. For the living out of the Triune fellowship takes place not only inside Adam's skin, not only inside the domain of evil, but also inside the covenant between God and Israel. The incarnation means that the relationship of Father and Son in the Spirit has invaded the human side of the covenant, set up shop inside Israel and Israel's side of the relationship, inside Israel's failure to answer the call of God.

In Genesis 3, God calls Adam and Eve, and they are hiding in the bushes unable to answer his call, unable to step forward and live in fellowship with God. That call echoes throughout the whole history of Israel without answer. It echoes throughout your life and mine without answer. But now, on the human side of that call, inside our failure to answer, stands the incarnate Son of the Father, the beloved Son as man. As he lives out his sonship, he is answering the call of Genesis 3. He is fulfilling the covenant, he is cutting into flesh and blood existence a real answer to the call. Step by step, blow by blow, through 33 years and a crucifixion, he answers the Father with all of his heart, soul, mind and strength. And he does so inside Adam's failure, Israel's failure, our failure to answer.

What does the incarnation mean? What does it mean that the Son of God lived out his sonship as a human being? What does it mean that the eternal fellowship of Father, Son and Spirit has set up shop and worked its way out fully inside human existence? It means that the covenant relationship between God and Israel has, at last, reached fulfilment. And more than that, it means that the covenant relationship has been filled with nothing less than the relationship of the Father, Son and Spirit.[27] The great dance itself is now the content of the covenant between God and Israel, and in Israel, with the human race.[28]

This is not theory. Jesus Christ sits at the Father's right hand as man, as Adamic man, as Israel, as Man of the Covenant, and he lives in covenant faithfulness and covenant fellowship with the Father in the Spirit, now and forever. He is the new covenant between God and humanity, cut into human existence and abiding forever.[29]

THE MISSING PIECE:
THE INCARNATION AS CONNECTION

But we are still only scratching the surface of the meaning of the incarnation. When the Son of God became human and lived out his sonship as man, Adamic existence was crucified and born again and exalted into the circle, the bondage of evil was overcome, and the new covenant was cut into human existence. But if we stop here, we still have no gospel. For as yet, we are still on the outside looking in. We are, as yet, only spectators. If we stop here, we have only "the hooray for Jesus" model of Christianity. Hooray for Jesus, he has made it. He has walked through it all and lives now inside the circle. He is the new man. He is victor. He participates fully, unhindered, unencumbered, in the fellowship of the covenant. Great for Jesus. But what about us? Is that it? Was all of this hammered out through fire and trial so that we would have a great example to follow? Does the Bible leave us staring at the ascension wondering how we are going to follow Jesus? Or is there something about the incarnation yet to be discovered, a missing piece?

To this point I have talked about the incarnation from the vantage point of the Son living out his sonship inside human existence. But this Son not only knows the Father and shares all things with him in the abounding fellowship of the Spirit—this Son of God is also the creator of the universe. He is the one in and through whom all things were created.

Remember that God *is* Father, Son and Spirit. There was never a time when there was just God. God has always been Trinity. There has never been a thought of God that was not Trinitarian thought. And there has never been an act of God that was not the act of Father, Son and Spirit. The Father never acts behind the back of the Son and Spirit. The Father does not have his "own thing" happening on the side, so to speak. He does not create the universe behind the back of Christ, without Christ's knowledge and without his participation. Creation is the act of the Father, Son and Spirit.

The New Testament is quite clear that all things were created not merely by God, but in and through and by the Son. Nothing, John says emphatically, *not one thing*, was created apart from the Son. It is in and through and by the Son that creation comes about, and he is the one in whom all things exist and hold together.[30] And that means that there is a connection between the eternal Son of God and all things. There is a connection between the eternal Son of God and every human being.

I have stressed that when the Son of God became man, he did not give up his Father. The fellowship of Father, Son and Spirit was not broken up and lost in the process. The Son did not cease being the Son. In the same way, we need to see now that when the Son became human, he did not cease being the One in and through whom and by whom all things exist. The connection between the Son of God and the cosmos, the universe, and the human race did not suddenly evaporate when he became a man.

When the Son of God stepped out of eternity into history, the connection between himself and the human race was not lost; it was tightened. It was solidified, made stronger, secured. That means that while Jesus Christ is a real man, an individual human being, he is also more than this. He is *the man*, the one man in whom the whole human race is bound up.

The history of Jesus Christ is therefore not just another event in a series of important events in human history. The history of Jesus Christ is *the* event of all events. It is *the* moment of all moments. What happens here in this God, what happens here in this Son in and through and by whom all things exist, is of fundamental and decisive significance for you, me, the human race, and indeed the whole cosmos.

For good or ill, what happens to this One, happens to us. For good or ill, what becomes of *him* becomes of the human race.

If *he* goes down, the cosmos goes down. If *he* dies, then we die.

And that is exactly what happened. The incarnate Son died, and in his death Adam died, the old man died,[31] you died, we died.[32] For it was no mere man who died on the cross. It was the incarnate Son, the One in whom all things exist. He was crucified, and in his crucifixion, Adam, you, me, the whole human race was crucified. God not only did something *for* us in Jesus Christ, God did something *to* us and *with* us. In Jesus, in this incarnate Son, God was acting upon us all, doing something to us, making something of us.

If the human race fell in a mere man named Adam, what happened to the human race in the death, resurrection and ascension of the incarnate Son of God? Why is it that the Church has been so quick to give Adam such status in the whole scheme of things and so slow to recognize the surpassing greatness of Jesus Christ? Is the incarnate Son less than Adam? Is Jesus Christ less a factor in human existence? Adam is only a man, a mere shadow when compared to the incarnate Son of God.

If we all went down in Adam, we certainly all went down in Christ. But that is only the beginning of the story. For the incarnate Son not only died, he rose. What happened to us in his resurrection? When this Son rose, did he leave us in the grave? Did he leave Adam behind? Did he leave you and me, the human race, in the grave? "Blessed be the God and Father of our Lord Jesus Christ," Peter says, "who according to his great mercy has caused us to be born again to a living hope through the resurrection of Jesus Christ from the dead." [33]

When this Son went down, we went down. And when this Son came forth from the grave, the human race came forth with him, quickened with new life, born again in the Spirit into a living hope. And when this Son ascended to the Father, he took the whole human race with him. [34] And there and then the human race was welcomed by the Father, accepted, embraced, included in the great dance.

A while back I was teaching on this connection between Jesus Christ and the human race, and when I finished, a young girl came down the aisle crying. I thought at first that I had said something that had broken her heart. I asked her what was wrong. She said:

> Nothing is wrong, Mr. Kruger. When you were telling your story, God gave me a vision. I saw God sitting on a throne, and there were all of these steps leading up to his throne. And there were people, hundreds and hundreds of people, on the steps. We were all trying to get to God, but none of us could make it. We kept falling, and we could not get to God, and we were all sad. And then I saw Jesus. He walked over and gathered us all up in his arms and he walked up the steps and put us in the Father's lap.

That is the missing piece of the gospel puzzle, the full meaning of the incarnation and ascension.

The gospel does not leave you staring into heaven wondering how you are going to make it like Jesus did. The gospel does not leave you now with yourself and with figuring out how your human existence is going to be converted, how you are going to gain victory over evil, how you are going to become a member of that new covenant fellowship that Jesus has with his Father. The gospel is the news that Jesus Christ has done it.

The gospel is not an invitation. The gospel is a declaration of the truth. It declares to us that we have been recreated in Jesus, that we have been delivered from evil in Jesus Christ, that we have been given a new relationship with the Father in Jesus Christ. The gospel declares to us that in the incarnation, life, death, resurrection and ascension of the Son of God, we were taken down and cleansed of all alienation; we were refashioned, recreated, born again; and we were lifted up into the circle of life shared by the Father, Son and Spirit, and there and then included in the great dance of the Triune God. Because it was no ordinary man who died and rose again and ascended. It was the incarnate Son of God, the one in and through and by whom all things exist.

3

THE RIVER RUNNING THROUGH IT ALL

The Trinity and the Secret of Life

The central affirmation of Christian faith declares that God himself has entered into our human situation and in doing so has totally transformed it. —A. M. Allchin[35]

I believe in Christianity as I believe that the Sun has risen, not only because I see it, but because by it I see everything else. —C. S. Lewis[36]

What are we to make of the fact that Jesus Christ is seated at the right hand of God, the Father almighty? What are we to make of the fact that he is seated at the Father's right hand, now and forever, not only as the Son of God but as the Son of God incarnate, and therefore as a human being? What are we to make of the fact that he is seated there not merely as a man, but as *the* Man, the Last Adam, the One in whom the whole human race is bound up? What are we to make of the fact that he has already included us in the great dance?

THE LIGHT OF THE WORLD

In John's gospel, Jesus declares: "I am the light of the world."[37] He does not say, "I will be the light of the world when people finally decide to follow me" or "I will be the light of the world when people finally get their religion right" or "when the Church does her job and converts the world." He says, "I *am* the light of the world." This is not a prophecy or a projection of what may be some day in the future. It is not even an invitation. It is a simple declaration.

The foundation upon which Jesus is speaking is the fact that he has done something that has changed the world. Quite apart from our consultation or consent, the Son of God laid hold of the human race and decisively altered its very identity and existence. He took us down in his death. He crucified Adam, you, me, the human race, cleansed us of all alienation and converted us to his Father. He lifted us up in his resurrection, gave us new life, new birth—recreated us in the Holy Spirit. He exalted us in his ascension and took us home inside the circle of the very life and fellowship and joy and glory of the Triune God. Jesus, therefore, does not present himself to us as a theory, a mere possibility, yet another potential truth among a series of potential truths for the human race: He presents himself as the light of our lives, as the mystery, the secret of human existence.

When Jesus declares, "I am the light of the world," he is not being arrogant, and he certainly is not being exclusive. He is telling us that he has already done it, that he has already drawn us within the circle. He is telling us that he has already included us in the great dance. Our inclusion, therefore, is not a goal that we must now achieve, or attain, or make true. It *is* the truth. And as such, it is the greatest of all clues as to who we are and what is really happening in our lives.

The fact that Jesus Christ is who he is and has done what he has done for us, with us and to us, means that there is already more going on in your life than you ever imagined. It means there is already more of the great dance about us than we have ever suspected. How could it be otherwise? If he shares in the life of the Trinity, and we are included in him, then it is impossible that that life is absent from our lives.

Jesus is not up there in some celestial sanctuary waiting for us to get our act together. He has not vacated the premises and left us as orphans,[38] outside the circle of his family life. He is not absent, he is present. And the one who is present is the incarnate Son, who shares all life and all glory and all fullness and all joy with his Father in the fellowship of the Spirit. The one who is present is the incarnate Son, the New Man who is face to face with the Father; the Victor, who lives beyond evil and darkness; the Covenant Man, who lives in unhindered fellowship with the Father.

The mystery at work in the universe, the light of life, the secret,[39] is that Jesus Christ is already sharing his life with us. The great dance is already afoot in your life and mine. In all humility and graciousness, Jesus Christ is already sharing his joy, his fellowship, his freedom with us. He is already sharing his glory and fullness and burdens with us. In all humility and graciousness, he is already sharing his creativity, his knowledge, his interests and clean conscience with us, his love. This is not theory, this is not a dream, this is the light of life, the mystery of our existence, the fundamental truth of things. Our job is to rethink everything we thought we knew about ourselves and others and what is going on in human life. For we have been given a staggering gift.

THE SECRET OF HUMAN LIFE

Just the other day, I saw a grandmother holding her baby granddaughter. She was standing in a restaurant in the Mall. I watched her eyes as she looked at that baby. I saw the love and the joy, the tenderness and the commitment. I saw the hopes, the dreams, the desires. I saw the laughter. I thought to myself. "Does all of that originate with that grandmother? Is she the one who creates that love, that joy, that tenderness, that commitment? Does it have its origin in her heart? Is that a mere human event, a mere human love? No, *that* is the great dance of Trinity at work within us, present, not absent."

There is only one circle of love in this universe, only one circle of life and fellowship and passion and tenderness and commitment. And that circle has been opened in Jesus Christ, and the human race, including that grandmother and that baby, have been taken into it. There is far more going on in her life than she ever imagined. More than likely, she is clueless about what is happening. More than likely, she thinks that it is all just human. But it is not "just human." It is the fellowship, the joy, the life, the love of the Father, Son and Spirit being played out in her and in her relationship with her granddaughter.

A friend told me that her church was studying spiritual gifts. She said the preacher listed all the gifts and gave everyone a form to fill out that would help them understand which gifts they had. She looked at me and said, "Baxter, I finally decided that I just did not have any spiritual gifts." I was shocked. For it was clear to me that she was blessed with the greatest of all spiritual gifts, and I told her so. I told her that she had the gift of hospitality. I pointed out how everyone who comes into the office complex goes straight to her desk and engages in conversation with her. Everyone is drawn to her. And I told her that without fail every conversation that I had had with her had left me uplifted and encouraged. She got a little embarrassed and said, "Well, I know that, but that is just me." And I said to her, "No, that is not just you. There is only one circle of hospitality in this universe and that is the circle of the Father, Son and Spirit. All hospitality, the spirit of all welcoming and encouragement and camaraderie and at-homeness begins there in the relationship of Father, Son and Spirit. You, my friend, have been included in that circle, and it is the hospitality of the Father, Son and Spirit that pours forth out of your being. The Father, Son and Spirit share their hospitality, their welcoming and quickening and encouraging Spirit, with the world through you."

This astonishing sharing is not a goal to be achieved. It is the way things are. It is the truth to be discovered, to be understood, the light by which we can finally begin to understand who we are and what is actually happening in our lives.

I saw a documentary not long ago about a rescue operation to save some stranded whales. It turned out to be a major project. I could not help but notice the earnestness of the people involved, the depth of their burden and commitment, their determination. There was certainly a lot of confusion in it, egos and pride and a definite air of superiority on the part of some. But the concern, the burden was unmistakable. I had seen that concern before. I had seen that burden in action before.

Who is it that cares about creation? Who is it that knows the stars by name, watches the sparrows and clothes the lilies of the field? Who is it that counts the number of hairs on each human head? Was the concern and the burden that drove the whole rescue operation all the way to its triumphant end merely human? Was the joy and the dignity and the camaraderie of it all solely a human affair? Are we to chalk this up to the innate goodness of human beings? I don't think so. There is only one circle of interest and concern and burden for the creation in this universe. And that is the circle of the Father, Son and Spirit. What my family watched on the television was nothing short of the Triune God in action, the Father, Son and Spirit tending to creation in and through the hearts and hands and feet of a group of human beings.

Let me give you another example of what I mean from my own life. One of my passions is fishing. A few years ago I started fiddling with the idea of making lifelike fishing lures, lures that look just like real bait fish. I worked for hours and hours in my shop, carving and sanding, trying to figure out how to put a shiny surface on the wood, how to give it scales and an iridescent hue, and how to paint it so that it looked real, how to give it lifelike action, even to the point of inventing a patented tail. The first lure was so ugly, I was embarrassed to show it to anyone. But I tried it out secretly, and on the second cast I caught a 6.12 pound bass. I knew then that I was on to something. So I pressed on until I got the lures to look and act the way I had dreamed.

One day my daughter Laura came out to the shop while I was putting the finishing touches on one of the lures. She stood there and watched for a while and then asked: "Dad, how did you ever come up with the idea of making these lures?" She was asking me about the creative idea itself and about all the little bits that go into the lure—the carving, the painting, the eyes, the tail, the iridescence. I turned to Laura and told her that I have a friend who loves fishing, all kinds of fishing, and when I get around him, he shares his ideas with me. In fact, it thrills him for me to take his ideas and carve them into being, so to speak. She asked if she knew my friend. I told her that she did, and she immediately started reeling off names. To each name I shook my head, saying that that was not the friend I was talking about. I finally told her that this friend loves music as well and cooking and laughter and gardening and baseball and animals. She paused. And then she asked, "Dad, you are talking about Jesus, aren't you?"

"Yes, Laura," I said, "I am talking about Jesus. The music that you play on your piano and the joy that you know in playing are not yours. They are part of the great dance of life shared by the Father, Son and Spirit, and Jesus shares them with you. He puts his music into your heart and you get to play it."

That is the light of life. Behind it all is Jesus and his life with his Father in the fellowship of the Spirit. He shares his ideas with us, his joys and delights and loves, his burdens and interests. He shares his life with us and we are living it out. The great dance is being played out every day in our lives. Our inclusion in the great dance is not a goal. It is not something that we must attain or achieve. It is the way things are. It is the light of the world, the secret of human existence, and all creation groans for us to see it.[40]

CONFUSION AND THE TRUTH

There is a sense, of course, in which our participation in the great dance is a goal. We are not computers with divine software. We are distinct persons who have been included in the great dance. As distinct persons, it is possible for us to become confused about who we are, and in our confusion go about things in the wrong way, which stifles our life in Christ. If we do not know who we really are as participants in the life of the Trinity, we get very proud of ourselves and what we think *we* have done, and that sanctimonious pride repels people and short-circuits the fellowship of the Trinity at work within us. If we don't know the truth, we become confused and believe wrong things about God, about ourselves and others, and in that confusion act in such a way that throws a wet blanket over our participation in the great dance. For example, if we do not know who we are in Christ, we fall into believing that our life and joy and fullness come from things, or from money, or from social acceptance or position. So we pursue these things and almost destroy our marriages and relationships, and the lives of other people, and the creation itself in the process.

Clearly, there is another factor in the equation of our lives, a sinister and dastardly factor, besides the reality of our inclusion in the Triune life. And we must sort it all through. We must understand who it is that confuses us and throws us into such darkness. And we must understand the logic of confusion, how it works and what it does to us and how it perverts our participation in the great dance. But we are in no position to undertake such a thing until we are squared away on the facts. It is only as we understand who we are in Christ that we have light to understand what is wrong and how to fix it. Only as we see ourselves not outside but inside, not excluded but included, not alone but bound up in Jesus Christ, do we have the light which exposes the deep lie of evil—that we are separated from God. And only then can we see how that lie operates in our lives.

First and foremost, we must be squared away on the fact that our inclusion in the great dance of the Trinity is not a goal for us to attain. It is the way things are. And we must learn to see ourselves and others for who they really are—not merely human beings doing their own things, but people caught up in the fellowship, the camaraderie, the glory and joy and love and life of the Father, Son and Spirit.

THE TRINITY, FARMING, AND BUILDING A LAKE

Last year I was going to speak at a college in the midwestern United States. A young man picked me up at the airport and we started driving through the countryside. For miles there was nothing but farms. We passed field after field, and in each field there was at least one, if not two or three farmers plowing. The student told me that after his college studies, he hoped to go to seminary and eventually into the ministry. I immediately asked him about all the farmers we had seen and specifically how Jesus related to what they did with their lives, the hours and hours that they spent on those tractors, plowing and planting and harvesting. He said that he had never really thought about that. I thought to myself, "Here are men who spend 60 or 70 hours a week, if not more, farming, bringing forth food for millions of people, food for which many will give thanks to God. Here is a good evangelical Christian student with eyes set on the ministry, and yet he has never thought about how Jesus relates to those farmers—to whom, in all likelihood, he will be ministering the gospel."

In the summer of 1999, I was involved in building a 39-acre trophy bass lake. I was hired as a lake design consultant by a friend who was heading up the whole project. The project itself was a huge undertaking, mind-boggling in fact. First there was the idea itself, and the hours and days spent searching for the right piece of land. Then there was the design of the overall project, the master plan—the engineering, the roads, the lots, the water supply and sewage requirements. Then there was the design of the lake, with its trenches and mounds and stump fields and delicate balance of spawning areas and various depths of habitat for the fish. Then there was the whole matter of financing the project. Hours and hours, day after day, of phone calls and research and planning and meetings.

When the day came to start work on the project, it was an incredible sight. Surveyors, engineers, dirt men, track hoe operators, bulldozers, dump trucks, loggers were all let loose on this parcel of land. Thousands of yards of dirt had to be moved. For the first several months, dump truck after dump truck hauled off dirt. Track hoes and bulldozers and scrapers worked from daylight till dark. Trees were cut and sold, some were pushed into huge piles in the lake bottom. Deep trenches were cut in the lake, mounds built, loads and loads of concrete pipe and riprap were hauled in. Day by day, the dam began to emerge, and the layout of the lots began to take shape.

I had the privilege of being in the middle of it all for several months. I watched the project move from head to paper to earthed reality through the hard work of men and machines. It was always hot. There was always sweat and frustration, something was always going wrong or breaking down, but in it all and through it all, there was an unmistakable joy. Grown men worked their fingers to the bone, every day, day after day, covered in dust and grease and grime. But to a man, they loved their work. Somehow they knew that in spite of the fact that they did not hold high-powered executive positions, what they were involved in was important, real, valuable. Almost every day I thought about the fact that in the near future the project would become a neighborhood with houses and children playing and people enjoying the great fishing—and some pausing for a moment or two to say thanks to God for such a place.

One day I was talking with the dirt man, the man in charge of everything that had to do with dirt, from the roads to the trenches in the lake, from the lot lines to the dam. I liked him immediately. He was loud, opinionated, and full of life. I don't know that I have ever met a man who loved what he did so much. We were taking a break from the heat and discussing some of the design features of the lake. He asked me what I did for a living. I knew the minute I told him that I was involved in ministry, the whole discussion would be over. So I came at it from the back side. I told him I was a writer. Of course he asked me what I wrote about. I told him that I was working on a new book about how God related to this lake project.

He was stunned, and he looked at me like a cow staring at a new gate, to borrow an expression from Luther. He asked me what on earth I was talking about. So I launched into my explanation of how God was not a boring old religious type up there in heaven watching us to see if we keep His rules. God lives as Father, Son and Spirit in a circle of creative life and fellowship and joy. I quickly moved into the second part about how what we are all doing in this project is participating in that creativity and fellowship. God does not need us to think up this lake or to design it or to finance it or to build it. The idea, the design, the thought, the work all begins with the Father, Son and Spirit. But, while the Father, Son and Spirit do not need us, they love to share what they are doing with us, to include us in their plans, and give us a place in their projects as the hands and feet and dirt movers.

That was as far as I got, for the dirt man cut me off and launched into his own sermon. He caught the vision immediately and was off and running. He said that he understood what I was saying and had always suspected that this was the truth of things. He did not necessarily understand the Trinity, but he instinctively understood the idea of participation and the dignity and joy of it all, and he knew that this joy and dignity had their origin outside of himself.

The next day, I took the kids to school, and as we waited in the car line, a milk truck passed us and pulled over to a side door of the school. A middle-aged man jumped out of the cab and all but ran around to the back of his truck. As best I could tell he was whistling. I watched him unload crate after crate of milk and orange juice. Again a sequence of questions rolled through my mind: "Is that man no more than the Eveready Energizer Bunny, a robot of sorts that God made and attached a battery to, turned on, and let loose to do his own thing? Is that just a man, just a middle-aged man making a living, or is there more going on here than meets the eye?"

God does not need this man to deliver milk. He does not need dairy farmers or the farmers who grow the food for the dairy cows. For that matter, he does not need dairy cows. He does not need the crate designers or the glass manufacturers or the automobile workers or the men in the Gulf who work on oil rigs to produce the gas to run the truck. He does not need mechanics to keep the truck in working order or the countless secretaries to keep everything organized and scheduled. He does not need the teachers to teach or principals to administer the schools or the cooks to cook the lunches or the maintenance men to keep everything running. He does not need the policemen to keep the traffic flowing and in order. He does not need the smiling lady who greets the kids as they get out of the cars. He does not need the countless radio personalities to make us laugh or the musicians to entertain us while we wait. He did not need the engineers and architects to design the school or the workers to build it or the loggers to cut the trees or the concrete men to make the blocks or the truck drivers to drive the cement trucks. He does not need the lady who toils, day after day, cleaning and cutting chickens to feed the children. He does not even need husbands and wives to make the babies. It would be no trouble for the creative power of the Father, Son and Spirit simply to speak, and it would all be so. But the Father, Son and Spirit are all about fellowship and shared life, and God delights in including mere humans in his work. And there is far more going on in an ordinary moment of an ordinary day on this planet than we have ever imagined.

Some of the men working on that lake project and most of the people whom I saw the next day as I dropped the kids off will no doubt go to church Sunday. And I'll bet that most will leave the church feeling guilty because they are not doing enough for God.

THE INCARNATION REVISITED

We need to go back to the incarnation. We have seen that the incarnation of the Son of God means, first and foremost, the coming of the Triune life of God into human existence. It was not just God, a bare and abstract divinity or divine power, who became man. It was the beloved Son, the eternal Son of the Father. And it was not just any divine life that set up shop inside human existence. It was nothing less than the eternal divine life of the Father, Son and Spirit. What entered into our world and into our human existence in Jesus Christ was nothing less than the great dance of life shared by the Father, Son and Spirit. The life of Jesus Christ is, first and foremost, the living out of this Trinitarian life inside human existence.

We have also seen the living out of this Trinitarian life inside three specific contexts: Inside Adam's skin and thus inside human existence as it has been devastated by the Fall; inside the domain and confusion and harassment of evil; inside the covenant relationship between God and Israel, and particularly inside Israel's failure to answer God in covenant faithfulness and fellowship. And in addition, we have seen how the living out of the Trinitarian life of God inside these contexts meant war, pain and suffering and tears on the part of the incarnate Son, but in the end, it meant the great conversion of Adamic human existence to God, full and complete and living victory over evil, and the fulfilment of the covenant fellowship between God and human beings.

But now we must go back and look at the incarnation, the living out of this Trinitarian life, one more time. We must go back and pay attention once again to what happened when this great dance of life shared by the Father, Son and Spirit set up shop and worked itself out inside human existence. At the very least, what we discover, when we stop to think about it, is that there was a moment in human history when carpentry was more than a mere human enterprise.

What are we to make of the fact that as the Son of God lived out his sonship, his divine life, he did so as a carpenter? Think of the hours and hours spent in the shop, the years of apprenticeship, the days and months and years hammering and cutting and carving and sanding. What are we to make of the fact that the vast majority of God's time on earth was spent in such ordinary, mundane activity? Have you ever thought about that? Most of God's time on earth was not spent in what people call "full-time" ministry. The incarnate Son spent more time making things with his hands than he did preaching.

When you stop to think about it, when the Trinitarian life of God worked its way out in human existence, it was all very ordinary. I am aware of the supernatural things that happened in Jesus. I am aware of the astonishing miracles. But I would hazard a guess that the Son of God ate more meals than he performed miracles. I know that the incarnate Son healed the sick, but I also know that he made a lot of tables. He had a lot of conversations with regular people, grew up in a family with brothers and sisters and cousins, celebrated birthdays and went to parties.

For at least a moment in history, human laughter, human sharing, human compassion, human love, human fellowship and camaraderie and togetherness were all more than human. For at least a moment in history, carpentry and the delight of making things and helping others, human excellence and the pride and joy of creativity and design and moving from design to completed product, were all more than merely human. They were the living expression of the humanity of God, the living expression of the incarnate Son living out his divine sonship, the living expression of a man utterly baptized in the Holy Spirit.

IS THE INCARNATION OVER?

The good news is that the incarnation is not over. The Son did not go back to some kind of bodiless non-human divine state at the ascension. He did not leave behind the robe of his humanity when he ascended to the Father. Today, and for all eternity, he lives as the beloved Son of the Father *incarnate*. Today, and for all eternity, he lives out his sonship as a human being. Today, and through all eternity, Jesus Christ shares in the great dance as a man. *And* he does so not just as any man, but as the mediator. He shares in the great dance as the one in whom the whole human race is bound, as the point of connection, as the union, between the great dance of the Triune life and human existence. He continues to live out his sonship, today and forever, as a human being—he just does not do it *alone,* but in union with us, in and through us, in and through our work and play and gardening, in and through our relationships, our friendships, our marriages and romance, in and through our doctoring and teaching and carpentry, in and through our lake designing and dirt moving, in and through our social work and research and study and saving whales.

It is just too human for us to understand, too close, too real, too ordinary for us to see it. Jesus has been turned into such a spectator, who watches us from a distance, that we have no idea who we are and what is happening in our ordinary lives. We are so busy searching for the supernatural, we cannot see it when it is staring us in the face. Do we honestly believe that our love for our children, our delight in flowers and gardening, our creativity and insight, our concern for others and our tears have their origin in our own hearts?

Several years ago I stood on the mound pitching baseball to a dozen little boys. Most of the boys did not know much about baseball, but they were caught up in it. I could see the eagerness in their eyes, the determination. I saw their camaraderie and fellowship. And I loved being in the middle of it. But inside of me there was a little wrestling match going on. One part of me was thrilled, the other part of me felt guilty. At the time I was a pastor, and I felt guilty that I was having so much fun doing something so secular. I should be praying for people, visiting the sick or working on my sermon—at least talking to these kids trying to get them saved. Right in the middle of that wrestling match, the Lord spoke to me. Baxter, don't you dare miss this. Don't you dare miss what is happening here on this field with these 12 boys. Baxter, there is more of my glory here, more of my life and the fellowship I share with my Father, more of the Spirit of sonship, and the free-flowing dance of the Trinity on this field, than you have ever seen in those sterile church services. Baxter, do not be blind. The great dance is present, not absent.

Jesus Christ is indeed living out his sonship, his great dance of life and fellowship with his Father, his baptism in the Spirit, but he does not live it out alone, he lives it out through us and through our ordinary human lives. And *that* is why we love life so. That is why we love baseball and gardening, fishing and cookouts and having coffee together. That is why we love lake designing and building projects. That is why we love laughter and fellowship and romance and sex. That is why we love adventure and racing cars and taking care of animals. The Father, Son and Spirit do not live out their great dance of life without us. The great dance of the Triune God is the river running through it all. And it is good.

CHRISTIAN FAITH

Christian faith is not something we do that gets us connected to God or gets us into the circle of life shared by the Father, Son and Spirit. Jesus Christ has done that. Faith is not something that we do that moves us from the unforgiven column to the forgiven column. That was done in Jesus. Faith is not something we do that gets us reconciled, justified, included, adopted, redeemed, saved. Jesus Christ has already done all of that. The fundamental character of Christian faith is that of discovery. Faith, as Luther said somewhere, is like the eye. It does not create what it sees; it sees what is there.

Christian faith is first and foremost the discovery of what the Father, Son and Spirit have made of the human race in Jesus Christ. Faith is the discovery that there and then in Jesus Christ we were reconciled, saved, adopted; there and then in Jesus Christ we were cleansed and born again, recreated and taken home to the Father; and there and then in Jesus Christ we were welcomed by God the Father almighty, embraced, accepted, included in the circle of life. Christian faith is first and foremost a discovery of truth in Jesus, the truth about God and the truth about ourselves, the truth of our identity, of who we are, a discovery of the fact that the Father, Son and Spirit do not live out their dance of life without us.

And that is a discovery that commands us to believe it as truth and to rethink everything we thought we knew about ourselves and others and our lives and theirs. That is a discovery that commands us to live in the dignity and joy and freedom of the truth and to recognize no one according to the flesh, as Paul put it,[41] as a "mere human." For, as Lewis says, "There are no *ordinary* people."[42]

4

LEGENDS IN OUR OWN MINDS

The Darkness and How the Dance is Distorted

So many people walk around with a meaningless life. They seem half-asleep, even when they're busy doing things they think are important. This is because they're chasing the wrong things.
—Morrie Schwartz[43]

The life of man becomes an unbroken chain of movements dictated by his anxious desire for assurances...
—Karl Barth[44]

Behind the universe and the human race lies the astonishing philanthropy of the Triune God. In sheer grace the Father, Son and Spirit have chosen not to live out their great dance of life without us. They have chosen not to hoard their glory, but to share it, to share their fellowship and camaraderie, their love and laughter, their creativity and dignity and excellence with us, to live it all out in union with the human race.

The great dance extended to us in Jesus Christ is the secret of our motherhood and fatherhood, of our loves and delights and joys. It is the glory of work, of building lakes and painting houses, of grocery shopping and cooking supper. It is the joy of baseball and the soul of everything good in life, of music and laughter, of friendship and fellowship. The great dance of life shared by the Father, Son and Spirit is the mystery moving behind the scenes of our lives, the invisible river running through our souls and through all things.

I have stressed that this is not a goal to be achieved or a dream to be attained. It is the way things are. There are not two worlds or two human races, one that was created by the Trinity and shares in the great dance and another that is just human, ordinary, secular. There is only one human race, and that is the human race that has been drawn within the circle of the Trinity in Jesus Christ. There is therefore nothing ordinary at all about our human existence. It is permeated with the relationship of the Father, Son and Spirit.

This staggering gift, this union, this life shared with us in Jesus Christ, does not mean that we become God or that God becomes us. That would be our ruin, for it would mean that we have become so absorbed into God that there is no "us" left to share in the dance. That is the perennial problem of pantheism—it collapses the connection between God and the world into a single entity, such that the world, for all practical purposes, vanishes. Human beings lose their distinct personal identity as a drop of water does when it falls into a river. On the other side of the coin is deism, which separates God and human beings. Whereas pantheism loses the distinction between God and the world, deism loses any meaningful connection or relationship between them. With deism, God is a spectator watching us from a distance, and human existence is merely human, and thus truly empty and meaningless and temporal. With pantheism, human beings are not much more than computers with divine software. With deism, we are mere variations on the theme of the Eveready Energizer bunny, except at some point our battery will die.

The interesting thing is that both pantheism and deism end up with the same disaster—a humanity that is truly lost, either by radical separation from God and thus eventual non-being, or by total merging with the divine and thus eternal bliss, but bliss *we* will never know. It is the genius of the Trinity to figure out a way to give us a real place in the Trinitarian life without losing us in the process. We are connected with the Trinity, but not absorbed; united, but forever and irreducibly distinct. We are thus neither computers nor independent biological life forms. We are genuine participants in the life of God.

Without this union, the human race would simply evaporate, and so would everything good and noble and beautiful about human existence—all love and passion, all creativity and joy, all adventure and learning, everything. The union, forged in Jesus Christ, gives us a place in Trinitarian life, and thus we are alive and there is a real life for us to live. And the distinction means that there is a genuine "us" here to experience it. It was a lavish and brilliant move on God's part. And apparently, given that the divine desire was to extend *the dance* to *us*, the only move to make. But it was also a move riddled with risk.

Whereas the union gives us existence and a place in the great dance, and the distinction means that there is an "us" around to taste and feel and know it, the distinction is also the crack in the door that can let in the snake. Without the distinction, everything is so merged into God we all lose our personal identity. So the distinction safeguards our genuine participation. But the irreducible distinction also sets up the possibility of our missing the point. It establishes the possibility of confusion on our parts, serious confusion, wrongheaded believing, and thus the possibility of the perversion and adulteration of our true being and life. It is possible, because we are genuinely distinct from God, for us to be so confused about who we are that we unwittingly work against our very beings and do violence to them.

The great problem that we face as human beings is not that we have been left out of the circle, rejected or abandoned or excluded from the great dance of life. For in Jesus Christ the Triune God has searched the universe for us, and found us, removed all alienation and brought us home. The great problem we face is the possibility of *darkness* and what darkness does to our participation in the life of the Trinity—what we do to the great dance in our darkness.

THE SINISTER PLOT

In the original preface to *The Screwtape Letters*, C.S. Lewis says that human beings make two mistakes about the devil. We either discount the notion of the devil, or of evil, as being mythical or primitive, or we pay far too much attention to it.[45] As far as we know, the devil is a fallen angel and is real, not real as the Father, Son and Spirit are real, but real as in dangerous to you and to me. In the end, the devil is no more than the Wizard of Oz, an old man working a great illusion. But it is an illusion which can and does enslave us all and wreak utter havoc in our lives here on earth.

It is inconceivable, but the evil one hates the Trinity. He hates the great dance. And above and beyond everything else, he despises seeing the dance of the Father, Son and Spirit being played out on earth, in you and me. The goal of the evil one, of *Diabolos*, is to destroy the dance of life shared by Father, Son and Spirit on this planet.

The evil one cannot change the facts. He cannot reach into the circle and rip us out of the Father's arms. He is no equal to the Triune God. He cannot sever the union between us and the Trinitarian life forged in Jesus Christ. He cannot alter the connection. Neither can he create another human race which would be his and would exist without connection to the Trinity.

There is only one human race, and that is the human race bound up with the life of the Trinity in Jesus Christ. The evil one is limited to the possibility of perverting or distorting or poisoning our participation in the Triune life. And he cannot do that without our permission, without our decision, without our choice. His strategy is to confuse us so that we unwittingly, yet willfully, work and act against our participation in the great dance of life. His sphere of operation is the irreducible "you" and specifically, your mind. His schemes are calculated to deceive. And the exact target of his schemes is our understanding of who we are, our identity.

I can imagine a memo, in Screwtape fashion, sent out by Diabolos himself to all his underlings which says, "Whatever you do, make sure it works to blind human beings to their true identity. Let them pursue their notions of spirituality and talk about God, even about Jesus Christ, if they must, just don't let them see that Jesus Christ has laid hold of them and taken them to his Father. Don't let them see that he has drawn them within the circle and given them a place in the great dance. Keep them in the dark about their identity. When you confuse them about their true identity in Christ, they lose sight of their purpose, they lose sight of the meaning and dignity of their lives. Then you've got them. All you have to do then is make the suggestion that what they seek is here in this person, this new job, this promotion, this car, this money, this sexual adventure. Like a martin to a gourd, they will run straight into idolatry. And the glory given to them will be perverted into emptiness and strife, the great dance will be distorted, shut down."

Our great problem as human beings is not that we have been left out of the circle; our great problem is that we have no idea who we are and what has become of us in Jesus Christ. We have been duped, deceived about Jesus and about ourselves. We have been sold a bill of goods, lied to, confused. We have underestimated Jesus Christ. And as a result, we have misjudged who we are and what is actually happening in our ordinary lives.

Underestimating Jesus Christ, and thus misunderstanding who we are, has resulted in the transformation of the whole Western world into a culture of anxiety and grief. Those two misjudgments have sent Europe and America and Australia into a massive identity crisis and into a mad and frantic dash to invent a new identity. Those two misjudgments have left you with a deep and profound anxiety that has sent you on a journey to find yourself, and in the process you are missing your true glory and your true life in Christ.

The Western world is healthy, powerful, and educated. We are blessed with enormous conveniences and luxuries, the abundance of every conceivable good. But we have lost the freedom to enjoy any of it. We are so anxious and frantic, so busy trying to find ourselves and our purpose, we look over and beyond our true glory and never even see it, let alone enjoy it.

We are like the kid at the fair who suddenly realizes that he has been separated from his parents and is lost. He is in the midst of everything a kid dreams about—rides, games and prizes, stuffed animals, cotton candy—but he is so torn up on the inside he cannot even see the fair and has lost every shred of freedom to enjoy it.

Our great problem as human beings is not that we have been left out. Our great problem is that we have no idea who we are. A dastardly confusion has set in around us and we cannot see what is right in front of our eyes. Or we see it, but we cannot see it for what it is. That is why Paul prays in Ephesians 1 for the Father of glory to give to us the Spirit of revelation so that the eyes of our hearts may be enlightened, so that we can see, know, understand both who we are and the glory and dignity and fullness that has been given to us in Jesus Christ.

A TALE OF BLINDNESS

Let me relay a story from C. S. Lewis' novel, *Till We Have Faces*,[46] that will help us understand our problem. Lewis' tale is set in ancient times and revolves principally around two sisters—Orual and Psyche. They are princesses in the Kingdom of Glome, which is somewhere near ancient Greece. All is well in the kingdom. Life is good. But then there are a series of famines, and the Priest of the goddess Ungit comes to the King with the horrible news that Psyche must be sacrificed to the goddess.

Within a few short days, Psyche is drugged and the whole kingdom forms a holy processional to the sacred tree, to which Psyche is chained and left to be eaten by the shadowbrute. Several days later, grief-stricken Orual journeys to the sacred tree, determined to give Psyche's remains a proper burial. At length, she gets there, only to discover that there is no sign of Psyche. There is no blood, no bones, no torn fragments of clothing, nothing. She wanders away toward the river, grieving. There, under a leaf, she discovers Psyche's ruby ring. She picks it up and is trying to understand what it may mean when she hears a voice. She looks up, and there, just across the river, stands Psyche!

Orual is astonished. She does not know what to think. Could it be Psyche? No, it must be a ghost. But no, it is Psyche, radiant and beautiful, indeed more beautiful than ever. But it must be a dream, a terrible trick of the gods. Psyche is dead, eaten by the horrible shadowbrute.

Orual crosses the river and runs to embrace her sister. It is no dream—Psyche is alive and well. After a long embrace, Psyche tells Orual her story of how the god of the west wind saved her from the shadowbrute and brought her to be his bride and live in his grand palace. Orual, so thrilled to have Psyche back and assuming that the trauma has deluded Psyche, listens to her story as a mother listens to a tall tale of her son.

Psyche leads Orual a few yards away to sit in the heather. Ever the warmest of hosts, she serves a glass of wine to Orual, the choicest of wine in the most exquisite goblet. She asks Orual if she likes the goblet. Orual nods and Psyche gives the goblet to her as a gift. But the truth is that instead of choice wine and a gorgeous goblet, Orual only sees Psyche cup her hands and give her a drink of water from a pool nearby. She still believes Psyche is traumatized and is so thrilled just to have her back that she plays along. But Psyche's tale about gods and palaces and being dressed in the most beautiful gowns continues on and on. Orual sees no palace, no finery, only Psyche dressed in rags, not a splendid gown.

At length Orual can bear it no longer. If what Psyche is saying is true, then she is as blind as a bat, and has been all her life. So she accuses Psyche of playing a game with her and demands that her sister show her the palace.

Orual is mystified when Psyche responds to her demand with a charming nod and an eager smile. "Of course, I will.... Let us go in..." Orual lifts her hands in exasperation, as if to say, "Enough is enough!" But she bites her lip and decides to play along one more time and asks if it is far to the palace. With that, Psyche turns and stares in sheer amazement at Orual. "Far to where?" Psyche asks. "To the palace," Orual shouts, "to your god's house!"

"Orual," Psyche says, beginning to tremble, "What do you mean, is it far?" With this, Orual becomes frightened, though she still has no notion of the truth. "Mean?" she asks. "Where is the palace? How far have we to go to reach it?"

Psyche begins to cry. Through her tears and trembling, she stares hard into Orual's eyes. "But this is it, Orual! Can't you see it? You are standing on the stairs of the great gate."[47]

There the two of them stand, together beyond all dreams and against all odds. Psyche is real enough. She is no dream. But Orual sees no palace, no great stairs, no wine, no goblet, no gowns; only trees and heather and a pool and a few odd stones.

In deference to the rules of the gods, Orual has to camp across the river for the night. Just at dark she strolls to the river for one last drink and one last look through the mist across the water. And then, she says, "I saw that which brought my heart into my throat." Before her very eyes stood the palace, vast and ancient and beautiful, "wall within wall, pillar and arch and architrave, acres of it, a labyrinthine beauty."[48]

But the glimpse does not last. The great palace disappears from her sight, and Orual falls back into the sanity of her natural vision. In the end, in spite of her brief vision of the beautiful palace, and in spite of her clear knowledge of Psyche's life and radiance, Orual decides that Psyche is mad, and she leaves, headed back to Glome.

THE LOGIC OF DARKNESS

It would be difficult to imagine a more poignant or tragic scene. Orual was so close to the truth, yet so far from it. She was right smack in the thick of things, but she could never quite get it. Everything was so vague, so mysterious, so enigmatic, so abnormal to her, like an optical illusion appearing and disappearing at random. No sooner did she see it than it was gone, and she had no idea what made it appear or what made it go away or even if it was real.

It is critical to note that the problem here is not one of absence. The kingdom was very much present, and Orual was very much included in it. She could not possibly have been any closer to it than she was. But she could not see properly. She did not have the right kind of eyes. A sinister and diabolical veil covered her eyes.

In the Bible this is called spiritual blindness. It is a disorder of what the Bible calls "the eyes of the heart." It is a problem of discernment, an inability to perceive and understand what is actually happening in life. It originates not with us, but with the evil one. But the Bible tells us that we all suffer from this disorder. Every one of us suffers from the veil. We are Orual. We all suffer from acute Glomitis! We stare the glory of God in the face, but our vision is so skewed we never see it.

Our blindness is disastrous enough, but that is only the beginning of our problem. For we act out of our blindness. We live out of the way we understand things, out of our darkened understanding. We react and respond out of our confusion. And when we do so, the glory of God given to us, our life in Christ, our participation in the great dance, is distorted, stifled, misused. We do violence to our true lives without even knowing it.

What happens when we do not see our true glory in Jesus Christ? What do we do when we see ourselves alone, outside, when we have no idea about the real Jesus Christ or of the great dance and our inclusion in it? What happens when confusion sets in and we misunderstand who we are? A definite and discernible pattern of human behavior follows spiritual confusion. Confusion leads to longing, and longing leads to searching, and searching leads to inventing, and inventing leads to emptiness—greater and greater emptiness.

Within us all stirs an unrelenting desire to find home. We are made for the great dance and we know it, and we are riddled with an irrepressible longing for its joy. The longing seems inconsolable. It brews a quiet desperation within us, and the quiet desperation drives us into a search to find our true home. We are convinced that we are "not," and we are driven to find a way to "become." Most of us, I suspect, have no idea how deep and dear the search is to us or how it utterly drives us. But what happens when you cannot find what you are looking for? What happens when your search leads you down one dead end after another? It is then that we move from searching to inventing. For when you cannot find what you long for, you invent it. When you cannot see the glory that has been given to us in Jesus Christ, you set about to create a glory that you can see.

When you cannot hear the music of the great dance, you set out to write your own music. And what happens when our invented glory proves to be empty? What happens when our music does not lead into the real dance? We are left empty and sad and lonely, depressed and angry and cynical, and the great dance of life we have been given to share in is distorted beyond recognition.

THE DREAM

Let me relay a dream here that helps us see the logic of the way darkness develops. In the dream, virtually every day at noon, a tall, lean man about 55 with an immaculately groomed beard would make his way to the local park. There he would stand on a bare spot in the midst of grand ancient oaks and perform a ritual of the strangest, most bizarre, movements I have ever seen. It looked like a Barney Fife version of *tae kwon do* in slow motion. This went on for weeks. Gradually others began to join him, until one day it seemed as though the whole town was there, following his lead. The movements were still bizarre, but they were in unison, religiously so, which gave the ritual a kind of curious beauty.

At last it all got the better of me, and I walked over to talk to the tall man. I asked him what he was doing, what they were doing. He answered, not flippantly, but carefully, and with an earnestness that betrayed long and serious reflection, "We are trying to create life."

The answer caught me offguard, to say the least, and I did not have the presence of mind to respond. I simply walked away, feeling like you do when you hear a wonderful sounding sermon in church, but you can never quite get a handle on the point. My first direction of conscious thought was along these lines: Maybe I was missing out on something; perhaps the joke was on me. After all, who doesn't want to have *life*, and who is perfectly content with the way his life is going? Maybe this man knows something that I don't.

Upon further reflection, my mind focussed on the word "create." He had not said, "We are trying to understand life," or "We are trying to get to grips with how to live life." He had said, "We are trying to *create* life." This is a simple distinction, but an enormous one. To create a thing is of a different order altogether than understanding it or improving it. To create something means that it is not already here and that you are calling it forth or bringing it into existence. The thing is absent, and you want it present.

But what if the thing already exists? What if it is already here, and in overflowing abundance? What if the problem is not that the thing we desire is absent, but that we are blind to its presence? In the case of the tall man and his followers, what if the life they seek is already present, but they do not know how to see it? They cannot recognize it. What the man really needs is not a ritual of creation, but a new prescription for his glasses.

We are back to Orual and the problem of blindness, but with a new twist that is critical. What is revealed here is the series of tragedies that are generated because of what is never seen. The tall man does not see the glory of life all around him; he therefore designs a ritual that can create a life that he can see. And off he goes dedicating himself and his life to his noble ritual and drawing others into his insanity.

And what is it that is being created in this ritual? What is the ritual actually producing? Is it life? Is it the great dance? Is it the real glory? Or is it simply an illusion, a hologram, powerless activity? And what happens to the poor people who embrace the rhetoric and the illusion? What happens to the people who give themselves to participate in his ritual, who place their hope in it and give of their time and energy and effort? Are they ultimately given what they seek, or does the whole process leave them lost to the real thing, increasingly oblivious to the actual glory, and thus more and more empty and miserable?

The tall man is a parable of the human situation. When we do not see the glory, we invent one that we can see. And our inventions are no more than sophisticated holograms. They are not the real dingo. They do not lead us to experience the glory given to us in Jesus Christ. In fact, they work against our true life in Christ. They work against our participation in the dance of the Trinity.

Our inventions are more than just distractions. They exacerbate our blindness and create within us a rift between who we actually are in Christ and what we are making of ourselves. They create a profound incongruity within us, a spiritual schizophrenia. There is

the real "us in Jesus Christ," and now there is "who we think we are."
And there is our real life in Christ, and then there is the life that we
are trying to live. Each step we take in the pursuit of our inventions
deepens the incongruity. Each step into our bizarre ritual, in effect,
gives actuality and size and reality to our "false selves" and denies
and strangles and suffocates our "true selves." We create a legend in
our own minds, and we pursue it, which stifles the "real us" and our
"true life" and leaves us empty and sad and lonely.[49]

LIGHT FROM MRS. FIDGET'S DARKNESS

One of my favorite characters in C. S. Lewis' writings is a lady by
the name of Mrs. Fidget.

> I am thinking of Mrs. Fidget, who died a few months ago. It is
> really astonishing how her family have brightened up.... Mrs.
> Fidget very often said that she lived for her family. And it was not
> untrue. Everyone in the neighborhood knew it. 'She lives for her
> family,' they said; 'what a wife and mother!' She did all the washing;
> true, she did it badly, and they could have afforded to send it out
> to a laundry, and they frequently begged her not to do it. But she
> did. There was always a hot lunch for anyone who was at home and
> always a hot meal at night (even in midsummer). They implored
> her not to provide this. They protested almost with tears in their
> eyes (and with truth) that they liked cold meals. It made no dif-
> ference. She was living for her family.... For Mrs. Fidget, as she so
> often said, would 'work her fingers to the bone' for her family. They
> couldn't stop her. Nor could they—being decent people—quite sit
> still and watch her do it. They had to help. Indeed they were always
> having to help. That is, they did things for her to help her to do
> things for them which they didn't want done.....[50]

The problem of Mrs. Fidget was not marriage, not relationships,
not motherhood. The problem of Mrs. Fidget was the way she saw
herself.

The evil one had whispered into her ear that she was not special,
not acceptable as she was, not good enough. He whispered his lies
into her ear that she was on the wrong side of the door of glory
and life, outside, excluded from the real deal. And she believed his

whisper. She believed that she was "not." So she dreamed a dream of "becoming." What did she do? She invented an ideal, a legend in her own mind. She believed that if she could attain the ideal, *then* she would become, *then* she would be acceptable, *then* she would be alive with life, on the inside of the glory.

Do you see how that works? Mrs. Fidget did not love her family. She loved herself and her dream. It was not her family that meant the world to her; it was her ideal, her legend. She did not work her fingers to the bone for her family. She worked her fingers to the bone for her dream of becoming. Her vision meant everything to her, she was bound by it, in bondage to it. She dragged her family into her darkness, manipulated them to participate with her in her legend, regardless of what they wanted and needed. And the dance of the Trinity given to her and her family, their true glory, was poisoned, stifled, shut down, to the point that her family "brightened up" when she was finally gone.

MRS. FIDGET AND THE HUMAN RACE

Mrs. Fidget, like the tall man, is a picture of the human race, of you and me. What happened to her is a picture of what happens to us in our darkness. We fall for the lies of the evil one. We believe in his whisper that we are "not," not acceptable, not special, not significant, not inside the glory, not a part of the real deal, not alive with life, not yet "there." So we do what Mrs. Fidget did. We invent a glory, an ideal, a legend in our own minds, we dream a dream that we believe will give us life. We conjure up an identity that we believe will solve the riddle of our lives. The Bible calls it "idolatry," because what we are inventing is nothing short of a god of some sort that we believe will give us what we do not have.

Most people, I suspect, have no idea what is going on inside of them. They don't know about the whisper. They don't know about the deception, and they don't know they are trying to reinvent themselves and live legendary lives. And most people certainly don't think of themselves as being in bondage. Mrs. Fidget didn't. She had convinced herself that she was living for her family. But she was not.

She was living for her dream and, in the process, shutting down the dance of the Trinity given to her and her family.

A young woman gets married with stars in her eyes. Without knowing what she is doing, she is investing all her hopes in her husband. She has believed the lie that she is "not," and she is turning to her husband and their marriage to "become." She is inventing a relationship that she believes will make her alive and imposing that legend upon her husband. At first he does his best to meet her needs, as most young husbands do. It makes him feel great to be so needed. He gives it all that he has. But it is strangely never really enough. It never really works. For the first few years, he tries harder, and she continues to hope that things will eventually change—that their marriage will become what she has dreamed it to be. But as time goes on, he feels incredible, unbearable pressure. He feels trapped. Whatever it is that he is supposed to be for her, he cannot be. She feels unimportant, undervalued, slighted, and thus angry and frustrated. The dance is short-circuited.

In all likelihood, she takes her sense of unimportance and anger into her motherhood and other relationships and to work, and it would not be far-fetched to think of her projecting her husband's inabilities onto every other man, tarring them with the same brush, so to speak, and thus sowing the seeds of darkness everywhere. Similarly, the young husband takes his feeling of inadequacy to work, and it translates into a relentless need to justify himself, either through performance or making more money, or expanding the company. And suppose he is in management and is charged with overseeing a sales force of 50 or so. It is not difficult to see how a little strategically placed lie wreaks havoc in a marriage and rolls like a tumbleweed through human lives.

The problem is not marriage. The problem is that we are the kid at the fair and we turn to a legendary marriage to be our salvation. We are Mrs. Fidget. And when we impose our legends, our dreams of becoming, our secret agendas onto our relationships, when we manipulate people to participate with us in our legends, the real relationships are frustrated, the fellowship is short-circuited. The dance is shut down.

The Western world is full of grown men who have no idea who they are. They have been lied to, and they believe they are "not." And they have dreamed a dream of becoming. They have invented a legend, a false glory. They have turned to work, more than likely, as the thing that will make them somebody, give them dignity. And it means so much to them, they are consumed with it. When they are home, they are not home. They are present physically, but they are so bound up in their dream of becoming, they are so preoccupied with their legendary work, they never notice the joy of God written into their daughter's heart. They never know their sons. They never see their wives for who they truly are. They play golf every Friday afternoon as a matter of ritual, but they are so driven they never really *play*. And what happens when they are up for promotion and someone else gets in the way?

A few years ago, a kid actually murdered his friend over a pair of Nike basketball shoes. I do not know the specifics of that horrible tragedy, but I know who is the source of all murder. The evil one is behind murder, in all its forms, whether it is by imposing our dreams upon others, or gossip and slander, or betrayal, or stabbing someone in the back at work, or literally by taking someone's life. The road to the kid's act of murder and every murder begins with the whisper "I am not."

Somewhere along the way, the kid believed the lie of the evil one that he was "not." And he dreamed a dream of becoming. He invented a legendary self. The only identity he could find was through the marketing hype of a corporation. He believed in the shoes. It was all he had. He believed they could give him an identity, make him special, make him "somebody." And the belief was so strong, the spiritual pain behind it was so acute, and the desperation was so deep he was prepared to do anything, even kill his friend, to get those shoes.

That is the logic of darkness. It begins with the whispering lie of the evil one, "I am not." And we believe his lie and become Orual, the tall man in the park, Mrs. Fidget. We dream a dream, we invent a glory, a legend in our own minds, and work our fingers to the bone to attain it, all the while not only missing our true glory, but unwittingly poisoning it, short-circuiting the life of the Father, Son and Spirit, the great dance given to us, doing violence to our very beings.

Mrs. Fidget and Western Culture

Mrs. Fidget is not only a picture of human beings, she is also a picture of Western culture. Underneath all the greatness of the Western world lies a profound crisis of identity, a crisis of meaning, purpose and dignity. We lost the Trinity. We lost the real Jesus. All we had left was the bare, abstract God, and Newton finished him off when he thought up his mechanistic universe. When that happened, God became a spectator, and we lost the secret of our identity and our reason for being on earth. So Western culture embarked upon a mission to invent a new identity, to create a new life, to manufacture meaning, to dream up something that would confer significance and glory upon us. We spend millions of dollars inventing legendary Olympic Games and Super Bowls and World Series in a mad and desperate attempt to manufacture glory, and never see the eternal glory of our children's very existence. Untold hours and dollars are spent creating the illusion of fame, which is then paraded before us as the height of glory, yet it never crosses our minds that God the Father almighty knows our names and likes us.

The history of the modern Western world can be written as a long and desperate search that has birthed a series of ingenious inventions which have entertained us and distracted us for a moment or two, but have never satisfied our hearts, never delivered the real glory. Moreover, they have left us increasingly oblivious to our true life. Modern Western history is a tale of a hurting soul inventing gods and goddesses, power games and illusions of grandeur; bizarre ritual after bizarre ritual; and endless, endless hype to convince ourselves that what we have invented is real.

We have everything, but we are bored stiff with it all, burned-out and profoundly apathetic. What we have on our hands today in the Western world is a culture of grief. We know deep inside that we have missed the great dance, and we are grieving the loss. That is good. For it means we are seeing through what we have invented. We are feeling its emptiness and meaninglessness. It means that we are one step closer to crying out for light. And that is the first step out of Glome.

Mrs. Fidget and the Church

Mrs. Fidget is a picture of human beings, of Western culture, and she is also, sadly, a picture of the Church. The Church is supposed to see the glory and know how to live in it. But the Church is as blind as the world, and because the Church does not see the glory, it has set out to create a glory that it *can* see. And then it takes all the great Bible terms—the kingdom of God, salvation, abundant life, baptism of the Spirit—and confidently pastes them on the side of its invented glory. Untold energy is spent desperately trying to convince itself and others that what it has invented is real. And anyone who dares raise a question about its invented glory is utterly shamed for disturbing the peace and unity of mother Church.

But what happens to the poor people who work the program, who do the Church thing, who follow the blind man in his bizarre religious ritual? Do they find the river, the dance, the glory? They are left sad and empty and bored and angry and depressed, and most seriously confused about Jesus. What happens to little boys and girls who know in the depths of their souls that there is a river of glory running through life and are told that this thing that the Church has invented is the river?

The Western Church faces a new problem these days, the likes of which it has never faced. The problem for the Western Church today is that people have done what the Church told them to do, they have done what the preachers told them to do, they have followed the program, the bizarre religious ritual with its Bible labels. And they have found no glory, no river, no great dance. Everyone in the Western world seems to know this but the Church.

People are not listening to the Church. And it is not because they hate God. It is because they have listened, and they have done what the Church told them to do, and it has left them empty. Could it be that the Western Church today is filled with people who know better, but prefer denial to the pain of facing their religious legends, and thus the pain of finding their way to the real glory? Could it be that the disinterest of the world in Christianity is owing to the fact that the world sees that denial and the religious nothingness it produces and wants nothing of it?

THE HOPE OF THE WORLD

Is it possible that the Father, Son and Spirit are standing by watching all of this with indifference? Is it possible for the Spirit of adoption to watch the human race flounder so in the darkness when it has been included in the great dance? I tell you the Spirit cannot bear it. He cannot bear to see you and me becoming Mrs. Fidget. He cannot bear to see the creation of the Triune God distorted beyond recognition. He cannot bear to see us living like the tall man in the park, falling for the lie of the evil one and spending our lives following some legendary glory, working a bizarre ritual that is destroying us.

The Spirit of adoption, the Spirit of truth, has been let loose upon the world, upon you and me.[51] And he comes to teach us, to enlighten us, to bear witness to the truth. He comes to help us see through the darkness and see who we are in Jesus Christ and comprehend the astonishing gift we have been given in him. In coming to help us discover the truth, he works to expose our stupidity, our bondage, our self-destructive entrapment in the darkness, to walk us through the pain of acknowledging our legends and their destruction.

The hope of the world, the hope of your life and mine, is that the Holy Spirit is the Spirit of adoption, the Spirit of truth, the Spirit of the eternal purpose of the Father and Son, and that he has an everlasting passion that we experience the great dance. Therefore he comes to us to strive with us and our wrongheadedness, to invade our confusion, our legends, our inventions, to lead us to proper believing, to train us to see through the darkness. He comes to teach us how to detect the whispering lie, how to discern good and evil, how to stand up to "I am not" and speak "Yes, I am" back to it, and how to walk and live in its freedom. He comes to lead us to discover the truth, to acknowledge it, and to reckon on it

The Father, Son and Spirit have chosen, in sheer grace and in astonishing philanthropy, not to hoard their glory and fullness and joy and fellowship. They have chosen not to live out their dance of life and glory without us, without you and me. But we have been sold a bill of goods, lied to, duped about Jesus Christ and about ourselves. We are profoundly confused about it all, and we are unwittingly doing violence to our participation in the dance. The Spirit of adoption cannot bear our confusion. So he has come to us to liberate us, and he will not let us go—until the earth is full of the knowledge of the Lord as the waters cover the seas.[52]

IN OUR RIGHT MINDS

Faith and the Release of the Dance

... There is a fire in the soul that comes from beyond and what the soul does in this life is very much driven by that fire. —Ronald Rolheiser[53]

Carry on, you will always remember, Carry on, nothing equals the splendor. Now your life's no longer empty, surely heaven waits for you. Carry on, my wayward son, For there'll be peace when you are done. Lay your weary head to rest, Now don't you cry no more. —Kerry Livgren[54]

Before the universe came to be, before the heavens were called forth with stars and moons, before the earth was carved in infinite beauty and human life was fashioned with style and grace and glory, before there was anything, there was the great dance of life shared by the Father, Son and Spirit. In staggering and lavish love, this God determined to open the circle and share the Trinitarian life with others. As an act of mind-boggling and astounding philanthropy, the Father, Son and Spirit chose to create human beings and share the great dance with them.

It was never intended that the fulfilment of this plan would be left in Adam's hands or ours. From the beginning, from before the beginning, the gift was given in and through Jesus Christ.[55] He was always destined to come and work out our adoption.[56] And that is what happened. The Son of God stepped out of eternity into history and carried out the eternal purpose of God for us.[57] Jesus has done it.

We have been blessed, Paul tells us, with every conceivable blessing in Jesus Christ. The very life of the Triune God, the communion and fellowship, the eternal joy and fullness and glory of the Father, Son and Spirit have been given to us. The great dance is now ours, as much as God's. It is the invisible river running through our lives and through all things. The beauty of a given morning, the smile of a daughter saying everything that needs to be said, a cup of coffee with an old friend, the passion of love, the peace of fishing in the shadows of a dying day: It is all poetry in motion—the great dance being played out through the scenes of our lives.

THE POSSIBILITY OF JOY AND SORROW

There is a voice, however, which mocks all this talk of a great dance. "Dance, what dance? Life is a bitch, then you die. It is a cruel joke, a pointless string of years riddled with tragedy and tears and unbearable sorrow. We are on a ride we did not choose, and we would just as soon get off." People are quick to think ill of others and just as quick to devastate the heart with hate and cruel words. For every fleeting moment of joy, there are hours of anxiety and depression. Fear rules. Chaos abounds. Jetliners crash, or are bombed out of the skies, leaving wives and husbands and children stranded on the shores of loneliness. Women are raped and brutally murdered. Tens of thousands of children starve to death before they turn three. Hurricanes rip miles of coastline to shreds, destroying houses and homes and hearts. Racism enslaves and crushes body and spirit. Children are beaten and abandoned. Corporations devour the earth and people. The average marriage, if it doesn't end in divorce, becomes a stalemate of mere toleration. For every good relationship, there are a thousand bad ones. For every smile of a daughter, there are one hundred frowns. Dance, what dance? It is the dream of fools, the blind romantic who refuses to see. Life is a sad and tragic tale.

Yet we know better. In spite of disappointment, in spite of heart-rending tragedies and deplorable injustices, in spite of times of untold grief and sorrow, and moments when the anxiety of it all reduces us to total silence, in spite of all the pain, we know that we are made for glory. The very things that mock the dance as the dream of fools, speak a double message. For even in their mocking, they are confessing that the great dance is no dream at all. Even tragedy itself shouts that we belong to the circle of life. For tragedy would not be so *tragic* to us, unless somehow we knew that we are made for glory. Is not tragedy defined as missing the good in a terrible and unfair way? Why are we troubled by injustice, unless we know that it is not the way it is supposed to be? "It is just not *right*," we say, but who told us it is not right? How can there be a "right" or a "wrong," a "good" or a "bad," or "a way it is supposed to be," and thus heartbreak and despair when it is not so, if the New Covenant is not written upon all our hearts? Our anxiety tells us that life is unpredictable and scary, but it also tells us that we believe it is supposed to be good, and that we are afraid of missing out on something that is ours. After all, we cannot be homesick if we have no home. We cannot be disappointed or frustrated or anxious if we are not convinced, in some deep way, that we're made for higher things. What is it that makes sorrow so sad and full of bitterness, and loneliness such an intolerable thing? How can we know misery *as misery*, unless we are made for the great dance and know it?

If we are convinced of anything as human beings, it is that the experiences of joy and sorrow are real, and so are the range of emotions that those two words gather up—satisfaction and frustration, hope and despair, laughter and crying, pleasure and pain, excitement and boredom, peace and anxiety, to name a few. We need no argument to convince us that these things are real. We have tasted them and felt them in our own hearts. But given that our experience of joy and sorrow are real, the question is, What is the basis for their reality? Have you ever thought about that? Most of us take if for granted that we are alive and that we feel the whole range of emotions. We never really think about the origin of joy and sorrow or how it is even possible for us to experience such things.

Is joy an airborne microbe, an emotional virus of some sort, which mysteriously floats into our lives and attaches itself to our hearts for a while and then leaves? Is sorrow an invisible dandelion, which just happens to cross paths with our souls while it wisps aimlessly through space? How is it possible for us to experience joy? How is it possible that we experience gladness and love, peace and hope? What accounts for the real presence of delight and pleasure and good cheer in our lives, or of laughter? On the other side of the coin, how is it possible for us to hurt? What accounts for the presence of anxiety and sadness and despair in our lives? Either joy and sorrow are both, in the end, complete illusions, pure figments of our imaginations, or they are real experiences. It seems the most obvious thing in the world that they are real, but where do they come from?

Our human experience of joy and sorrow is rooted in the reality of the union between us and the Trinity. The connection forged in Jesus Christ is real, and it has given us a definite identity, a nature, a home. We belong, from soul to body and from head to toe, to the Trinity. The dance is ours—we are wired for it. Its logic is our spiritual DNA. And on some deep level, we know it. We know that the great dance is ours. We are not only wired for it; its rhythm beats in the marrow of our souls. We are thus not neutral creatures. We are bound up with the Father, Son and Spirit. Paradoxically, it is this union, this belonging, this home in the Trinity, and our deep-level knowledge of it, that make both joy and sorrow possible for us and so *real* to us. The union defines the landscape of our lives. It is the unspoken standard by which our hearts measure all things. It is the stake in the ground, the bull's-eye, which defines the mark for our hearts. Sorrow is what we feel when we miss the mark. It is precisely because we are included in the great dance and know it, that to experience anything less makes us sad and frustrated and empty. It is because we are made for glory that to miss it hurts like hell, to find it is the highest of all joys.

Underneath our experience of joy and sorrow is the matter of our identity, of who we *are*, and of whether or not we are being true to ourselves. Delight and gladness, satisfaction and peace do not appear out of thin air, for no apparent reason. They are not airborne microbes. They are the fruit of living in accordance with who we really are. Pain and suffering, grief and anxiety are what we experience when we violate our identity. Joy is the name we give to the experience of living *in sync* with the life of the Father, Son and Spirit. Sorrow is the name we give to the experience of living in violation of that life. It may be that the cause of the violation comes from something we have done ourselves, or from something someone has done to us, or from the inexplicable accidents of chaos. But whatever the cause, the reason it disturbs us so and hurts so deeply is that it violates our beings. It is a breach of our identity. How could such a breach not hurt? How could there not be weeping and gnashing of teeth when we do violence to our very beings?

Just the other day I was fishing, and I was shocked all over again at the way a bass goes so berserk on the ground. To jerk the fish from the water is to remove it from its native environment, its home, and thus to violate its identity. How could it not go wild? It is made for water. To remove it is to throw it into contradiction, and thus torment. The fish needed no added whipping from me to suffer. And its release back into the water needed no added blessing from me to make it flourish.

This analogy of the fish is good, as far as it goes, but it is limited because it is spatial, not relational. The fish is "taken out" and put "back in" the water, and its suffering or flourishing is related to "where" it is. It is not so with us. We are not taken out or put back in. We are "in," now and forever. Jesus has accomplished that. And it is the fact that we are "in" that creates the possibility of real joy and sorrow for us—the highest joy and the deepest sorrow. It is the fact that we have a home in the Trinity that makes it possible for us to be so dis-eased, so uncomfortable with ourselves, so homesick and brokenhearted and despairing; or at peace and at-home and flourishing.

There is only one circle of life in the universe, and we belong to it. Thus, we are alive, and there is a beautiful life to live. But our belonging also means that there is a harmony that we can violate, a union that we can contradict. To do so hurts. It creates guilt and shame within us, a haunting sense of alienation and loss, and the first hints of deep sadness. And it creates these things in us because we are contradicting our very beings. We are going against the grain of our true selves.

The other side is equally true, and even more so. We belong to the Father, Son and Spirit; the rhythm of the great dance beats in our hearts. To walk to its rhythm is not to move to an alien beat; it is to hit *our* stride. It is to find *ourselves*. It is to find home and at-homeness, genuine fulfilment, and the first tastes of everlasting joy.

Let me relay a story here that helps us visualize the point more clearly.

LOST IN NEW ORLEANS

When I was 12 years old, my parents took me and my two brothers and my best friend to New Orleans to see the Minnesota Vikings play the Saints. Being from a small town in south Mississippi, I considered the chance to go to New Orleans a great treat in itself: But given that the Vikings were my all-time favorite football team, this trip was one of the highlights of my youth. The three hours it took to drive to New Orleans seemed to me an eternal day. But we finally got there, and my Dad parked the car. We took a trolley to the old Tulane stadium. It was a magnificent afternoon, and the game was everything I had dreamed it would be, including a Viking route.

After the game, we were walking down the exit ramp when I looked over the rail and saw three busses lined up, and I recognized the huge men boarding the busses as the Viking players themselves. Without thinking, I ran down the ramp and somehow made my way to the players. I actually shook hands with Carl Eller and was inches away from Alan Page and Wally Hilgenberg. And I got to touch Coach Bud Grant's hat. Needless to say, I was in heaven.

Then one by one, the busses began to drive away. I remember watching them go beside the stadium and turn left, out of sight. When the last bus was gone, the greatest of all fears seized my little heart. I suddenly realized that I had no idea where my parents were, and worse, that they had no idea where I was. I looked around and there was not another person in sight, not one. To this day, it is a mystery how the crowd around those busses disappeared so quickly, but they did. There was not one single human being to be found. Sheer panic gripped me. Within seconds, I was scared out of my mind. I did not have a clue as to what to do. My heart was racing so fast I could not even think.

Twelve years old, New Orleans, Tulane Stadium, and it was getting dark. I was a long way from being street-smart, but I knew to the roots of my soul that I was in trouble. At some point it dawned on me to find a policeman, but there were none. I could not find another person, let alone a policeman, and I walked around that entire stadium at least three times.

By this time I was frantic and crying my eyes out. There were plenty of houses around, but I was not about to go in one for help. The only thing I knew to do was to try to find my way back to the car. I thought of the trolley that we had taken to stadium, but which one? North and south were meaningless to me on the streets of New Orleans, and I had no idea which direction to go anyway. I did not even remember any street names. But I had some money in my pocket, so I found a trolley car and got on and told the driver that I was lost. He told me to get in the back of the trolley and keep my eyes peeled, and if I saw anything, to pull the cable and he would stop. As the trolley made its way around New Orleans, I jumped from one side to the other, pressing my face against the cold windows, hoping, just hoping, that I would see something that I recognized—a tree, a building, a street, a parked car, who knows—maybe even my parents. But it did not happen. I rode that car all the way around its circuit until it got back to the stadium. Not knowing what else to do, I got off and walked around the stadium all the way back to where the busses were. Alone and scared to death, I sat down under a oak tree in a pile of leaves. I remember fiddling with a stick and crying, but there were no more tears. It was pitiful.

But things got worse. As I sat there, my 12 years of life flashing before my eyes, the stadium lights suddenly went off. I have never experienced darkness like that. Nearly 30 years later I can still see the darting, haunting shadows of that place and still smell the concrete and hear the leaves rustling in the cold wind. I don't know how long

I sat there, but it seemed like hours, certainly longer than the eternal ride to the stadium. It was so dark. I was so alone and cold.

And then suddenly, the stadium lights came on, and before I knew what was happening, I was on my feet running around the stadium. Someone had to have turned the lights on, and I was determined with the fire of the universe to find that someone. And then it happened. Over the noise of my footsteps and the pounding of my fears, I heard the most blessed sound in all of New Orleans. It was the most blessed sound I had ever heard in my life: One word "Baxter!," shouted by my father.

No one had to tell me what to do. No one had to tell me what that word meant. No one had to tell me how to apply the word to my life. My name, shouted by my father, spoke the hope of a thousand volumes. As with a great geiser in Yellowstone National Park, the unbearable tension was instantly relieved. The overwhelming fear, the frantic searching took a left turn like the busses and were gone. And in their place arose the simplest and most wonderful of all things: security, assurance, rest.

Nearly 30 years have passed since that day. As I look back, it is clear that the tale is filled with lessons, the most obvious of which is the relationship between my identity and the experience of suffering and joy. I could not have been lost, and suffered all the pain of that lostness, if I had not had a home. It is precisely because I had a family, a mother and father and brothers and a friend, that my experience was so miserable. My *experience* of pain was owing to the fact that I belonged to a family and knew it. If I had been on the streets of New Orleans as a homeless street child, with no roots and no family, there would have been no such trauma. We cannot be lost if we have no home. And we cannot experience pain and sorrow and despair, unless at some deep level we know our home is real.

UNITED, BUT IRREDUCIBLY DISTINCT

The first thing to be said about our *experience* of joy or sorrow is that it is possible only because we belong to God, and because at some deep level we know it. The union gives us our identity, a home, a family to which we belong, a real place in the great dance, and thus a life to experience. But this union is only the foundation of our experience. Inclusion itself in the life of the Father, Son and Spirit does not necessarily generate the *experience* of peace or frustration in our hearts. We could be united with God in a pantheistic way and thus be so absorbed into God there would be no distinct "us" left to experience anything. We are back to the "irreducible distinction" between us and God that we talked about in the last chapter. The possibility of "our" experience of anything lies in our union with the Trinity, on the one hand, and in the real distinction between us that is wonderfully maintained in the union, on the other. Without the union, we would not exist, and there would be no life to experience. Without the distinction, there is no real "us" to taste and feel and experience the life.

But there is more to be said. While the the union and distinction between the Trinity and us create the possibility of our experience, they do not make our experience either good or bad. Just because we have a home, and a distinct mind and heart and will, does not necessarily mean delight or sorrow. Congruence and incongruence are what make our experience one of peace or turmoil. Confusion and clarity, harmony and disharmony with our own identity in union with God are what make the experience of joy or sorrow real to us.

The union between us and the Trinity forged in Jesus Christ is real. It gives us our existence and a life in which to share. The irreducible distinction between us and God assures that there is a real "us" to experience the shared life—to taste and feel and know it. Moreover, the distinction means that it matters what "we" do. We have distinct minds and hearts and wills, but they are minds and hearts and wills that exist in union with God. It is no light matter for our thinking to be in conflict with God's thinking. Such incongruence is a violation, not of some arbitrary and extrinsic divine law, but of our own identity in union with God, and it necessarily causes anguish. For our hearts to be at odds with God's heart is necessarily to experience the most profound dis-ease. It is a violation of the union, of our identity as those who are united with the Father, Son and Spirit. The same is to be said of our wills. It is painful for our distinct wills to be in conflict with the will of the Father, Son and Spirit, for our wills exist in union with the divine will. To disagree with Plato is no great matter. But to be in disagreement with Jesus Christ is a contradiction of our very beings. For we exist in union with Jesus. Such disagreement and contradiction necessarily produce pain.

The risk that God runs in giving "us" a "real place" in the great dance is the possibility of our dis-ease, of our pain and sorrow and depression—even our ultimate and eternal sadness and misery. The distinction between us and God is as real as the union. It creates the possibility of confusion on our parts. And it is confusion on *our parts*, confusion of those who are in union with the Father, Son and Spirit, that generates our misery and despair.

Without the union, confusion carries no necessary dis-ease. Without the union, there would be no uncomfortableness, no tears or sorrow or despair. We would never be touched by the smiles of our daughters or weep when their hearts are broken. We would never see the beauty of a given morning. A cup of coffee with an old friend would mean nothing to us, for there would be no friendship, no soul ties, no memories of shared joy. Without union with the Father, Son and Spirit, there is no life worth living—no joy, no fellowship or togetherness, no laughter or delight, no romance or love, no poetry in motion. But we are united with the Father, Son and Spirit. We belong to the holy Trinity. It is this belonging that gives such devastating power to confusion and such liberating power to clarity. Knowing the truth sets us free, as Jesus said,[58] precisely because it is "our" truth. In the same way, confusion produces sadness precisely because it is a violation of our very beings.

The idea of faith is not an arbitrary divine invention which has been imposed upon us to test us. The command of faith is written into our identity, and so is its necessity, and its power. What we believe matters because we are distinct from, yet *united* with the Father, Son and Spirit. The union means that our legends *are* legends, and that they hurt, for they are contradictions of our union with God. The union also means that there is a "right mind" for us to be in, and that being in our right minds releases the great dance in our lives. Were there no union between us and the Triune life of God, what we believe—whatever that might be—would have no power and no necessary consequence. Our believing could not produce any particular experience. It could not make us sad or happy. Without the union, our legends would be as valid as any other theory on life, and just as impotent. They would be mere theories, which could never touch our hearts. But we *are* united with the Father, Son and Spirit, our legends *are* violations of our identity, of who we really are, and thus they inevitably produce incongruence, disharmony of being. Even if punishment ever crossed the mind of the Father, Son and Spirit, there would be no need for it. For wrongheaded believing necessarily produces its own hell. In the same way, believing the truth needs no external reward. Believing the truth brings medicine to the soul, for it is an act of rationality, the alignment of mind, heart and will with reality.[59] Such alignment necessarily generates peace and wholeness, and releases the joy of the dance in our lives.

All of this is to say that it is precisely because we belong to the Trinity that what we think and do matters so much. If we were not united, we could believe whatever fanciful tale we wished and it would have no bearing upon us, because it would be neither a legend nor the truth. We could do whatever we wished and it would not trouble us. It would not make us happy or sad, satisfied or malcontented, thrilled or depressed. Likewise, we could try with all our might to make "faith" work, make it do something for us, produce some experience, some good result in our hearts and lives, and it would be utterly powerless. For faith without reality, faith without truth, faith without prior union, is merely another legend. It is the mere flexing of a muscle that is not attached to a body. To believe that we belong to the Holy Trinity gives us hope and assurance and peace, not because our faith is magic, but because we are believing the truth. If we did not belong to the Trinity, believing so would have no power whatsoever.

THE DEEPER KNOWLEDGE

But there is yet another factor that figures into our experience that needs to be highlighted. It is what we might call "the paradox of knowing." It is a strange thing, but we *know* and yet *do not* know at the same time. Think of a master chef creating a new sauce. First she has an idea, then she gathers all the ingredients she thinks she will need. Next comes the long experiment, the process of trial and error. At each step she stops and tastes what she is making, to evaluate and see how close or how far away she is from what she is after. At last comes resolution as the sauce in the pan matches the sauce in her mind.

The most fascinating thing about the process is the question, How did the chef know when her sauce was right? How could she evaluate what she was making? How did she know when it was off just a bit? Paradoxically, the chef was of two minds, or at least in touch with two knowledges. At some level she *knew* exactly what she wanted, and that knowledge functioned as the supreme taste bud, as it were, evaluating and passing judgment upon what she was making—declaring it to be off, not yet right. Yet on another level she *did not* know what she wanted. She had to learn by experimenting. She had to step forward and try something. She had to act.

The paradox at work in the chef is a variation on the theme of our lives. We live between knowing, yet not knowing; between knowledge of who we are, yet ignorance of how to be. Somehow we *know* who we are. At some deep level, we know that the great dance is no romantic theory, but our destiny. We know that we belong, that we have a home. And it is this deep level knowledge that functions as the supreme taste bud in our lives. It haunts us and passes judgment upon us. It evaluates what we are doing and thinking and believing. It is this deep level knowledge that the great dance is ours that creates the experience of both pain and joy. When the life we are living matches the life we know in our hearts, it gives us joy and satisfaction. When it does not, we are sad and empty and despairing.

THE WITNESS OF THE SPIRIT

But how is it that we know and yet do not know? The deep knowledge is the fruit of what is called "the witness of the Spirit." The Spirit bears witness with our spirits that *we are* children of God.[60] It is not an accident that the New Testament refers to the Spirit as the Spirit of truth[61] and as the Spirit of adoption.[62] On one level, the Spirit comes to us because of who he is and because of

98

who we are. Jesus Christ has included us in his relationship with his Father, and that is a relationship that has always been filled with the Spirit. In some beautiful and deep way, the Spirit is the "go-between God," to use John Taylor's phrase.[63] He is the one who facilitates the relationship, the fellowship and togetherness and love of the Father and Son. That does not make the Spirit less important; if anything, it makes the Spirit the *sine qua non* of the great dance. Without the Spirit, there is no relationship of the Father and Son, no connection in love, no camaraderie and togetherness.

All of this is to say that it is impossible for us to be included in the relationship of the Father and Son, and for the Spirit to be neutral towards us or absent from us. Pentecost necessarily follows the ascension. For the one who ascended is the one in whom the whole human race is bound. For him to step into the circle, so to speak, means that we too are included in the circle, and that means included in the Spirit. Viewed from this angle, the gift given to us in Jesus Christ is the gift of the Spirit. As the Spirit of the great dance, he is the Spirit of our lives, the life of our party.

But the Spirit is not vague. He is the life of the dance, but that life is always intelligent life, eloquent, always bound up with the living Word of the Father. The presence of the Spirit always speaks, always carries a message and conveys meaning to us. On the one side, the Spirit is the source of the animation of the creation—the life of all things. On the other side, his life always tells us something, bears witness with us that we are not our own, that we belong to God, that we are a part of a definite circle. The deep-level knowledge at work within us is the fruit of the Spirit. In and through him the great dance is shared with us, and the sharing of the dance always bears witness with our spirits that we are not our own, but belong to God. Because of the Spirit, we *know* who we are, and we are restless until the life we are living matches the life we know is ours.

THE LETHAL ROUX

We know that we belong to the circle of life and we know that life is good, and this deep-level knowledge evaluates our living, so much so that we cannot be content with anything less than the great dance. We are driven by our knowledge of the truth. It calls and commands and goads us. But paradoxically, we know the truth with confused minds. Like the chef, we know, but we do not understand. We are confused. It is this paradox of knowing and not knowing that drives the whole harrowing experience of human life. If we did not belong to the Trinity, we would be most apathetic and lifeless. But given that we do belong to the circle of life shared by the Father, Son and Spirit, and given that at some deep level we know it, the search for our holy grail is on, and whether we are aware of it or not, it is the only search that really matters to us. The trouble is, our holy grail is not a new sauce, but the consolation and resolution of our very beings, and the ingredients with which we are experimenting are not butter and garlic and wine, but our own hearts and the hearts of others, as well as the well-being of the earth. Our wives and husbands, our children and friends, our co-workers and our play, and our relationship with the earth itself are caught up in our trials and errors.

Behind our confusion is not ignorance, but the evil one, who lurks in the shadows of our lives whispering "I am not" to us. His whisper has no power in itself. It does not carry the weight of the witness of the Spirit because it is neither a divine word nor a word of truth—a word rooted in the way things are. The whisper is not the voice of authority, which stops us in our tracks and commands our attention. The whisper is fluff, a figment of the evil one's own bloated imagination. It is a lie, but we can believe it to be true. And even though it will forever be a lie, by believing it to be true, we give the lie a foothold in reality. When we believe "I am not" to be the truth, we give it a place in time and space, a place in our lives and in the lives of others. Without necessarily knowing what we are doing, we give the lie a place in our thinking, we open ourselves to its influence, and our understanding is darkened. A breach is formed, a fatal incongruence between who we are in our union with Christ—accepted, loved and included—and who we *believe* we are.

When we believe the evil one's lie "I am not" (which is, in essence, his own confession about himself whispered to us), a lethal roux[64] of insecurity and anxiety and fear begins simmering in our souls. And this lethal roux immediately permeates our entire lives. It flavors the way we see ourselves and everything around us. It shapes our perspective. What happens, for example, when we believe that we are not acceptable, not good enough, not special, not included, not beautiful? It is impossible to believe in such "notness" and remain calm, secure, assured. To believe that we are not included means that we believe we are outside the circle, excluded from glory and meaning, excluded from *life*—both in the sense of life as existence itself and in the sense of life as *alive,* full of animation and passion and joy. How could we possibly believe such things and remain peaceful? To believe that we are not included strikes fear in the core of our beings. It stirs the profoundest insecurity and anxiety within us. It transforms us into the kid lost in New Orleans.

When you are hungry, you go to the refrigerator and get something to eat. When you are sick, you go to the doctor. What do you do when your soul hurts and is riddled with insecurity and anxiety and fear? You try to fix it. Whether or not you feel the pain, your soul is consumed with finding a solution. So you find a trolley car and get on, hoping, just hoping, that you will see something or find someone who can speak assurance. You turn to your husband or wife or friends or work to fix the problem. You create a legendary life and set out to live it. Or you set up a legendary set of rules by which you seek to prove to your own soul that you are okay, justifying yourself against your deeper knowledge. Or you spend your time trying to deny that there is a problem at all. You see what happens.

The lie, and our faith in it, stirs the lethal roux into being, and we walk into the day, into our relationships with our wives or husbands or children, into the workplace or the golf course or the mall or the church, with a soul bleeding with anxiety and fear and insecurity, consumed with itself and its pain, desperate for a solution—absolutely driven to find something or someone who can give it assurance. The strangest thing of all is the fact that most of us don't even know we are hurting, let alone that we have become human vacuum cleaners in our neediness.

The whisper, and our faith in it, is the root of the grotesque tree of lust and greed, envy and gossip and slander, anger and depression and cynicism. Do you see how that works? To believe that we are "not" stirs the lethal roux into being, and that fear and insecurity and anxiety drive us to believe in something that will deal with the pain. And the evil one is there with his suggestions as to the solution. Whatever it is that we decide will help us becomes something for which we begin to lust. Our passion for the dance is translated into an insatiable craving for this supposed savior. And what happens when we cannot get to our savior, or when someone else gets to it before we do, or we get to it, at last, and it does not really deal with our pain? What happens when our legends prove false either as a result of personal experience or from someone exposing their falsehood? Before we know what is happening, we have spent 10 or 15 or 20 years moving from one thing to the next, moving from one savior to another, or desperately pretending that our particular legend is indeed the truth, and protecting it with a vengeance. All of this creates an ever-increasing contradiction between our true selves in union with the Triune God, and the life we are living. Such incongruence generates the pain and misery and emptiness of hell within us, as it is a violation, not of some theory of Plato or Kant, but of our very beings.

FAITH AND THE ROUX OF THE DANCE

But to discover the truth in Jesus Christ, to come to know him as the Lord and Savior of the human race, to see him at the Father's right hand and to see ourselves accepted in him, embraced by God the Father almighty, included in the circle of life, is to have our thinking turned inside out, fundamentally reordered into harmony with the truth. The New Testament calls such radical realignment, such renewal of our minds, "repentance" (*metanoia*). It is a profound change of seeing, of understanding and thinking—the healing of Glomitis. What does such a conversion of our thinking do to us? What happens to the lethal roux when we see Jesus Christ in his true glory and we see ourselves not outside, but inside; not excluded, but warmly and lavishly embraced, seated with Jesus at the Father's right hand—and we believe it to be the truth? What happens to the anxiety and insecurity and fear that percolate in our souls? And what happens to the legends and bizarre rituals that have grown up out of our blindness and the gut-wrench of the lethal roux?

To discover the truth about Jesus Christ and the truth about ourselves in him—and to believe it as the truth—is to have a different roux stirred into being in our souls. Not one of fear and anxiety, but one of hope and peace and assurance. This is the roux of the great dance. We walk into the day, into our relationships with our wives or husbands or children, into the workplace or the golf course, the mall or the church with souls full of hope, quickened with assurance and security and confidence, and thus not as human vacuum cleaners but as overflowing fountains, as rivers of living water, as Jesus described it,[65] which give rather than take, refresh rather than stifle. And what happens in the mix of such refreshment? What happens when we are freed from our self-centeredness, free to notice others and to care genuinely about them, free to listen and not to impose our own agendas, our legends, upon them? What happens when we are freed from the need to hide, and are thus free to know and be known? What happens when the grotesque tree begins to change and bear a different fruit—not lust and greed and envy, but love and joy and peace, patience and kindness and goodness?

It is clear why the New Testament is always talking about faith and repentance. Given what Jesus Christ has accomplished, given what he has done for and with and to the human race, given that he has connected us with the Triune life, everything now hinges on what *we* believe. To persist in believing in the lie that we are separated from God, and thus that we are "not," is to live with the lethal roux and its dis-ease and to be driven into self-centeredness and manipulation, hiding and loneliness. To believe the lie is to live in the *tear* between knowing we have a home, but never finding it; it is to live on the trolley car. But to come to believe in Jesus Christ, to see him as he is and to see ourselves included in him, is to come into our right minds. It is to have the tear healed, and with that healing, to experience resolution and peace, hope and assurance.

Several years ago I was having lunch with a group of men when someone told the inevitable joke about a genie and three wishes. As best I can remember, the joke was actually funny, for laughter erupted with such intensity that everyone else in the restaurant turned and stared at our table. As things quieted down, someone turned the joke into a moment of serious reflection. "What if," he asked, "we *did* have three wishes?" That question launched a long discussion about what really matters to us, in the midst of which someone boiled the three wishes down to one. "What if we had only *one* wish, what would it be?" I went to sleep that night thinking about that question and the answers that we had given, both the funny ones and those that were serious. It helped me peel the layers back and get to the heart of things. By the next morning I had come to a conclusion. My wish would not be for money or opportunity, or even health or love, important as each of these may be. If I had only one wish, it would be for assurance. Why assurance? Because assurance is the critical link between our inclusion in the circle of fellowship shared by the Father, Son and Spirit and its release in our lives. We can possess all things; we can have millions of dollars in the bank and be in perfect health; we can even be deeply loved and surrounded by great friends, and yet be so bound up on the inside, so afraid, so riddled with insecurity, that we cannot enjoy any of it. "What does it profit a man," Jesus asked, "if he gains the whole world but loses his own soul?"[66] The same question applies to families and nations.

Paul's famous triad—faith, hope and love[67]—far from being a bit of sentimental religion, actually unveils the way of the great dance. For faith in Jesus Christ produces hope in our saddened and anxious souls. And "hope" in the Bible never means a dream, as a young boy dreams or hopes of making it to the big leagues when he grows up. Hope means assurance, deep and abiding confidence that things will be alright. Such hope and assurance undermine our anxiety and insecurity and immediately stir real changes into being. The sheer relief that swept through my heart when I heard my Dad shout my name on the streets of New Orleans is a case in point. That is a picture of what faith in Jesus Christ produces inside of us. To believe in Jesus Christ is to hear the Father himself call our name, and to experience the relief and the life of that hearing.

Believing in Jesus Christ produces assurance in our innermost beings, and assurance changes us. To begin with, assurance changes our perspective. Anxiety makes the most beautiful of days appear gray and full of gloom; assurance gives us eyes to see it in its glory, for it calms our insides long enough for us to notice beauty. On another level, assurance wars against our insecurity, and in so doing relieves us of the pressure "to become." This relief in turn steals the lure and power of our legends and establishes a new-found freedom in us to let them go, to die to our legendary selves. On yet another level, assurance works against our preoccupation with ourselves, for self-centeredness is born of fear. Working on all of these fronts, assurance functions as a door which opens the way for the care and love and fellowship of the Father, Son and Spirit to move out from our hearts to others. As faith in the lie produces fear, and fear makes us self-centered, and self-centeredness short-circuits the dance, so faith in Jesus Christ produces hope, and hope frees us from ourselves to notice others, to care for them and give ourselves for their benefit, to love. In such noticing and caring and loving, fellowship is born, and in fellowship the great dance is realized in ever-increasing fullness.

From one angle, assurance is the key to the life of the Father, Son and Spirit reaching full expression in our lives and relationships. For assurance allows us to move out of ourselves in self-giving and self-sacrificing love. We are included in the fellowship and life of the Triune God, and our participation in that fellowship and life flowers as assurance rises in our souls. For assurance alone gives us the freedom to notice, to listen and hear, to know and be known. But underneath assurance lies faith in Jesus Christ. Assurance is not something that we can manufacture. It is the fruit of faith in Christ. It is only as we believe ourselves to be wrapped up in him and in his relationship with the Father that real assurance, with all of its freeing power, takes root in us. But as critical as assurance is, it is not the main point. Neither is faith. They are servants of a higher cause. They are not the prize, but the means to it. The prize is to experience the great dance in all its fullness and glory together. That happens as we die to our legendary selves and step forward in freedom to give ourselves for others in love. For self-giving love lies at the heart of the great dance of life shared by the Father, Son and Spirit, and certainly at the heart of its release in our lives and relationships.

THE RISK OF GOD AND THE PASSION OF THE SPIRIT

The risk that the Triune God runs in giving "us" a "real place" in the circle of life is the possibility that we will continue to live from our darkened understanding. The risk is the possibility that we will continue to choose freely, through our confusion, to embrace our legends and bizarre rituals—even the religious ones—and thus throw ourselves into contradiction, into the tear and its unimaginable sadness and misery, indefinitely.[68] Lost is defined not in terms of whether or not we belong to the Trinity, for that has been settled once and for all in Jesus Christ. You cannot be lost if you have no home. We belong to the Father, Son and Spirit. To be lost, therefore, is not to be cut out of the circle or excommunicated, for that is now impossible. There is no power in heaven or on earth that can undo the union forged in Jesus Christ. As long as the *incarnate* Son sits at the Father's right hand, we are included. For he is no mere man. He is *the man,* the one in whom the whole human race is bound up. Lost is thus defined not in spatial terms as being cut off or separated from God, but in relational terms, as being a matter of whether or not *we know* we are united, and a matter of what the lack of that knowledge does to us. To be lost is to be confused about our identity in union with the Father, Son and Spirit, so confused that we give ourselves freely to invent and "believe in" and pursue a legendary identity, and thus suffer the contradiction of our beings in union with the Father, Son and Spirit and with one another. The risk the Triune God runs is the possibility that in our real distinction we will choose to exist in such violation forever.

Over 1600 years ago, St. Athanasius wrote of the divine dilemma when Adam fell and the creation of God began lapsing into non-being.[69] In such a situation, the question was, "What then was God to do when His creation was on the road to utter ruin?" For Athanasius, the only possible answer was redemption. For God loved his creation. Therefore, he sent his son to lay hold of the creation and bring it back into the circle of life. That dilemma was solved in the death, resurrection and ascension of the incarnate Son of God. For he laid hold of the human race, and in his life, death, resurrection and ascension took us down and cleansed us of all alienation, brought us forth anew and lifted us up into the circle of the Trinity. But in so doing, a new divine dilemma has arisen. For in giving "us" a "real place" in the circle of life, the possibility is established of our wrong believing and thus of our living in the tear and contradiction and angst of confusion. For God to cross the boundary of our distinction and make our decisions for us, to believe for us, is no answer, for that would be our ruin. It would mean the end of our distinct minds and hearts and wills, and thus the end of "our" experience of the great dance. What then is God to do?

Is there a double risk here? Have the Father, Son and Spirit, in their extravagant and lavish love, hazarded their own joy for the possibility of ours? Could we be so united with the Trinity that to violate our union creates untold pain in us, and yet not so united that our pain touches the heart of God? If we are so made for God, as Augustine said, that we are restless until we find our rest in Him,[70] is God not so made for us in Jesus Christ, that He too is restless until we find our way home?

The fact that God is prepared to run such a risk speaks volumes to us about the confidence that the Father, Son and Spirit have in the sheer goodness of their shared life, and in the ultimate appeal and power of our real place in it. The deck is stacked in God's favor and ours. For it is not a matter of our choosing between two equal options. We are united with the Father, Son and Spirit, not with evil. The trinitarian life is our home, our family, our all. We are wired for the great dance and long for its fullness with the passion of the universe. We have no longing for evil or darkness. While we are certainly confused and locked in convoluted understanding, and while we bear the tear of such wrongheaded thinking and incongruence, our passion is for life, not death; the great dance, not misery.

The deep knowledge that we are made for glory is itself enough to goad us along the way, given time and experience. For knowing that we belong to glory means, at the very least, that we despise pain and thus run from it. But it does not necessarily mean that we run to life. We could run more deeply into our legends or invent new ones. So the Spirit of our adoption not only speaks to us across the boundary of our distinctness and bears witness with us that we are children of God; he also convicts us of our wrongheaded believing. He is at work leading us from false believing into right believing, and that means leading us into faith in Jesus Christ and in the truth about us in him.

This is the real story of our lives. We are united with God, but wonderfully distinct, and in our distinctness from God we are confused about who we are and driven to find resolution. The Spirit is at work leading us to the truth, but there are no instantaneous enlightenments. It is with our confused minds that we are being led to know the truth. It is not always readily apparent what is truth and what is error. The wilderness did not appear to be the way of liberation for the Israelites. There were times when the bondage of Egypt appeared to be more bearable than the wilderness, even more desirable. But in the end, the bondage of the lie is far more painful than the journey of liberation.

The Spirit is the master teacher. He has the truth, and just as important, he knows when to speak it. He is faithful to bear witness to us that we belong to the Father and Son, and faithful to point out our wrongheadedness. His witness evaluates what we are believing and doing. It is the supreme taste bud, which tells us that this or that is bitter or sweet. But we have investments in our legends, especially our religious ones, and do not want to let them go. So the Spirit lets the pain and bitterness of our legends move us to the point where our hearts and minds and wills cry out for light. As Lewis says, "Experience is a brutal teacher, but you learn, by God, you learn!"[71] The Spirit uses the trolley car to give us ears to hear and eyes to see. It takes time and experience.

From our vantage point, life is about finding the elusive holy grail. The deeper knowledge, shared with us in the Spirit, haunts us to the core of our beings and drives us to find and experience the life we know is ours. Our longing is, in actual fact, for the great dance and its release in the totality of our human existence, from our designing lakes and moving dirt to farming and gardening and golf; from our relationships with one another in marriage and family and friendship, to the relationship of the nations of the earth; from our little corner of the world to the whole creation. For that is who we are; we are all bound together in the circle of life shared by the Father, Son and Spirit, and that life is pressing for realization in us all. But we are so confused, we have no real idea what we are searching for, let alone how to get there.

It is true, as Vladimir Lossky says, "Between the Trinity and hell there lies no other choice,"[72] but that is exactly where we are— somewhere between the great dance and its ultimate distortion. We live between light and darkness, between right and wrong believing, between the lethal roux and the roux of the dance, as our souls wander inconsolably through life, turning over every leaf in our universe to find resolution.

From the vantage point of the Father, Son and Spirit, history— both personal and corporate—is about our education. It is about a long walk with us in our darkness and confusion and pain, an endless and patient act of self-giving love, which bears our suffering in its determination to bring us to our right minds. For behind our existence and that of the universe is the original decision of the Father, Son and Spirit to share what they have with us, and with that decision the unflinching, tireless determination that it will be so. In sheer grace we have been included in the divine family in and through Jesus Christ. From the moment of that inclusion through the rest of history, all the divine resources are dedicated to our enlightenment.

Our problem is not a lack of desire for life, but a profound confusion as to how to experience it. "Our hearts are good. It is our minds and feet that do not know which way to go."[73] We have been duped about God, about the Father, Son and Spirit, and about who we are in Jesus Christ. So duped that in our search for life, for real relationships, for community and fullness and joy we look beyond Jesus Christ as being irrelevant. Over against such confusion—and in, with and through it and its havoc—the Spirit is educating us, suffering with us as he patiently and carefully leads us to the truth as it is in the *real* Jesus.

We are not forsaken. God is with us, giving us a share in the circle of life and bearing the pain of our darkness in order to enlighten us. This is one of those moments in our history when we feel the tear between our true identity in Christ and the life we are living; one of those moments when our legends, both religious and cultural, have run their course and left us anxious and sad and miserable, and we are more alert, listening with a more careful ear, crying out for answers. And this is one of those moments when the astonishing philanthropy of the Triune God is being revealed all over again, and we are faced once more with the question of Jesus: "What do you seek?"[74]

> Now may the God of hope fill you with all joy and peace in believing, that you may abound in hope by the power of the Holy Spirit. (Romans 15:13)

NOTES

1. C. S. Lewis, *Mere Christianity* (New York: Collier Books, Macmillan Publishing Company, 1960) p. 153.

2. See his autobiography, *Surpised by Joy* (New York: Harcourt Brace & Company), p. 16.

3. See *Surprised by Joy*, p. 230.

4. From "The Shorter Catechism" in *The Constitution of the Presbyterian Church (U.S.A.): Part 1: The Book of Confessions* (Louisville: The Office of the General Assembly, 1991), 7.001-010. Note that George MacDonald loved this first question, but thought that the catechism was a disaster after that. One of his characters, Alec Forbes, put it this way: "For my part, I wish the spiritual engineers who constructed it [the shorter catechism] had, after laying the grandest foundation-stone that truth could have afforded them, glorified God by going no further. Certainly many a man would have enjoyed Him sooner, if it had not been for their work." Cited by Michael R. Phillips in his excellent biography, *George MacDonald* (Minneapolis, Bethany House Publishers, 1987), p. 82.

5. "The Larger Catechism" in *The Constitution of the Presbyterian Church (U.S.A.): Part 1: The Book of Confessions* (Louisville: The Office of the General Assembly, 1991), 7.117.

6. See James B. Torrance, *Worship, Community and the Triune God of Grace* (Downers Grove: IVP, 1996).

7. See Ephesians 1:3-5.

8. St. Irenaeus, *Against the Heresies*, book V, preface, in *The Ante-Nicene Fathers*, vol. 1: *The Apostolic Fathers with Justin Martyr and Irenaeus*, ed. by Alexander Roberts and James Donaldson (Grand Rapids: Wm. B. Eerdmans Pub. Co., reprinted 1987). Note also St. Athanasius' famous statement: "For He was

made man that we might be made God," *On the Incarnation of the Word* (*St. Athanasius: Select Works and Letters, Vol. IV* of *The Nicene and Post Nicene Fathers of the Christian Church*, second series, edited by Philip Schaff and Henry Wace [Grand Rapids: Eerdmans Publishing Company, reprint 1987]), 54.3. Note also his comment: "For that was the very purpose and end of our Lord's Incarnation, that He should join what is man by nature to Him who is by nature God, that so man might enjoy His salvation and His union with God without any fear of its failing or decrease, *The Orations of St. Athanasius Against the Arians* (London: Griffith, Farran, Okeden & Welsh), II.70.

9. See John 19:30 and 17:4.

10. For further study on this problem, see William C. Placher, *The Domestication of Transcendence* (Louisville: Westminster John Knox Press, 1996) and Michael J. Buckley's fascinating, yet heady, book, *At the Origins of Modern Atheism* (New Haven: Yale University Press, 1987).

11. Note that in the definition of God cited earlier from the Shorter Catechism the Trinity is not mentioned at all. In the next question, the catechism brings the Trinity into the picture, as if to correct itself, but that begs the obvious question, Why is the Trinity completely omitted from the first and more fundamental definition of God?

12. See Geoffrey Chaucer, "The Knight's Tale," in *Canterbury Tales* (New York: Washington Square Press, 21st printing, 1975), p. 25.

13. James B. Torrance, *Worship, Community and the Triune God of Grace* (Downers Grove: IVP, 1996), p. 21.

14. St. Athanasius "Against the Arians" in *St. Athanasius: Select Works and Letters, Vol. IV* of *The Nicene and Post Nicene Fathers of the Christian Church*, second series, edited by Philip Schaff and Henry Wace (Grand Rapids: Eerdmans Publishing Company, reprint 1987), II.70.

15. See Colossians 1:19 and 2:9ff.

16. Trevor Hart, "Humankind in Christ and Christ in Humankind: Salvation as Participation in Our Substitute in the Theology of John Calvin" (*Scottish Journal of Theology* vol. 42), p. 72.

17. See John 1:14.

18. Note C. E. B. Cranfield's comment on the meaning of the world "flesh" in his essay, "The Witness of the New Testament to Christ," in *Essays in Christology for Karl Barth*, edited by T. H. L. Parker (London: Lutterworth Press, 1956), p. 81. "The New Testament bears witness to a condescension of ineffable graciousness, the descent of the Son of God from the glory which He had with His Father before the world was, to the very lowest depths of human suffering and shame. This downward movement, indicated in 2 Cor. 8:9 by the pregnant expression

'became poor' and traced in more detail in Phillipians 2:6-8... was a real and thorough-going self-identification with sinful men. The words 'became flesh' mean that, without ceasing to be God, He took upon Himself not a human nature uncorrupted by man's fall, but the selfsame human nature that is ours, that is, a fallen human nature. It was with that altogether unpromising material—what Paul calls σαρξ 'αμαρτιας (Rom. 8:9)—that He wrought out His perfect obedience to the Father, being 'in all points tempted like we are, yet without sin'. 'Became flesh' and 'became poor' are not adequately interpreted unless we go as far as this."

19. Thomas. F. Torrance, *The Mediation of Christ* (Grand Rapids: William B. Eerdmans Publishing Company, 1983), pp. 48-49. Compare St. Athanasius' comment which is typical of the early Church Fathers: "As, on the one hand, we could not have been redeemed from sin and the curse, unless the flesh and nature, which the Word took upon Him had been truly ours (for we should have had no interest by his assumption of any foreign nature); so also man could not have been united to the Divine nature, unless that Word, which was made flesh, had not been, in essence and nature, the Word and Son of God. For that was the very purpose and end of our Lord's Incarnation, that He should join what is man by nature to Him who is by nature God, that so man might enjoy His salvation and His union with God without any fear of its failing or decrease," *The Orations of St. Athanasius* (London: Griffith, Farran, Okeden and Welsh), II. 70. For a scholarly treatment of Christ's assumption of our fallen humanity, see Thomas G. Weinandy, *In the Likeness of Sinful Flesh* (Edinburgh: T & T Clark, 1993) and Harry Johnson, *The Humanity of the Saviour* (London: The Epworth Press, 1962).

20. "Only if Jesus assumed a humanity at one with the fallen race of Adam could his death and resurrection heal and save that humanity" (Thomas G. Weinandy, *In the Likeness of Sinful Flesh,* Edinburgh: T & T Clark, 1993), p. 28.

21. "For in that act of incarnation we behold the nature of sinful, fallen, suffering man entering into sweet and harmonious union with the sinless nature of God....the most violent of all contradictions reconciled; and a door of hope, yea, and of assurance, opened, which no power shall ever shut" *The Collected Writings of Edward Irving,* ed. by G. Carlyle, vol. 5 (Alexander Strahan, Publishers, 1865), p. 327-328, see also pp 114-146.

22. As Thomas G. Weinandy puts it: "The eternal Son of God functioned from within the confines of a humanity altered by sin and the Fall" (*In the Likeness of Sinful Flesh,* Edinburgh: T & T Clark, 1993), p. 18.

23. Thomas G. Weinandy, *In the Likeness of Sinful Flesh* (Edinburgh: T & T Clark, 1993), p. 28.

24. See Hebrews 5:8.

25. See Mark 14:32ff.

26. John Calvin, *Institutes of the Christian Religion,* volume XX of *The Library of Christian Classics,* edited by John T. McNeill (Philadelphia: The Westminster Press), II.xvi.5.

27. Note T. F. Torrance's comment, " . . . in Jesus Christ the Covenant faithfulness of God has been met and answered by a Covenant faithfulness within our humanity, so that that divine-human faithfulness forms the very content and substance of the fulfilled Covenant which is the New Covenant. Thus the Covenant relationship is now filled with the relationship or communion between the Son and the Father, and it is in that communion that we are given to share by the Spirit" (*Conflict and Agreement in the Church,* [London: Lutterworth Press, 1960], vol. 2, pp. 122-123.

28. See Isaiah 42:6.

29. See Hebrews 8-10.

30. See John 1:1-3; Hebrews 1:1-3 and Colossians 1:16ff.

31. See Romans 6:6.

32. See 2 Corinthians 5:14ff.

33. 1 Peter 1:3.

34. See Ephesians 2:4-7.

35. A. M. Allchin, *Participation in God: A Forgotten Strand in Anglican Tradition* (London: Dartmon, Longman & Todd, 1988), p. 1.

36. C.S. Lewis, "Is Theology Poetry?" in *The Weight of Glory and Other Addresses* (New York: Simon & Schuster, A Touchstone Book, 1996), p. 106.

37. See John 8:12.

38. See John 14:18.

39. See Colossians 1:27.

40. See Romans 8:19.

41. See 2 Corinthians 5:16.

42. C.S. Lewis, "The Weight of Glory," in *The Weight of Glory and Other Addresses* (New York: Simon & Schuster, 1996), p. 39.

43. Mitch Albom, *Tuesdays with Morrie* (New York: Doubleday, 1997), p. 43.

44. Karl Barth, *Church Dogmatics* (Edinburgh: T & T Clark, 1958), IV/2, p. 469.

45. C.S. Lewis, *The Screwtape Letters* (New York: Simon and Schuster, Touchstone Edition, 1996), p. 15.

46. C.S. Lewis, *Till We Have Faces* (New York: Harcourt, Brace and Javanovich, Publishers, 1980). See also chapter 13: "How the Dwarfs Refused to Be Taken In" in *The Chronicles of Narnia*, vol. 7: *The Last Battle* (New York, Collier Books: Macmillan Publishing Company, 1956) and also Lewis' brilliant book, *The Great Divorce* (New York, Collier Books: Macmillan Publishing Company, 1946).

47. Lewis, *Till We Have Faces*, pp. 115-116.

48. Lewis, *Till We Have Faces*, p. 132.

49. Note Frederick Buechner's comment, ". . . we try to make ourselves into something that we hope the world will like better than it apparently did the selves we originally were. That is the story of all our lives, needless to say, and in the process of living out that story, the original, shimmering self gets buried so deep that most of us end up hardly living out of it at all. Instead we live out all the other selves which we are constantly putting on and taking off like coats and hats against the world's weather" (*Telling Secrets*, [San Francisco: Harper, 1991] p. 45).

50. C.S. Lewis, *The Four Loves* (New York: Harcourt Brance and Company, A Harvest Book, Reprinted 1991), pp. 48-50.

51. See John 16:7ff.

52. See Isaiah 11:9.

53. Ronald Rolheiser, *The Holy Longing* (New York: Doubleday, 1999), p. 16.

54. From the song "Carry On Wayward Son" written by Kerry Livgren on the CD *The Best of Kansas* (Sony Music Entertainment, Inc., 1999).

55. See 2 Timothy 1:9.

56. See Ephesians 1:3-5.

57. See Ephesians 3:11.

58. See John 8:31ff.

59. See Thomas Erskine, *The Unconditional Freeness of the Gospel* (Edinburgh: Waugh and Innes, 1829), pp. 13ff.

60. See Romans 8:16 and Galatians 4:4-6.

61. See John 14:27; 15:26 and 16:13.

62. See Romans 8:15.

63. See John V. Taylor, *The Go-Between God* (London: SCM Press Ltd., 1972).

64. "Roux" is a French cooking term for the thickening agent, made of butter and flour, used in sauces. In Cajun and Creole cuisine, the idea of "the roux" has evolved to include the blending of any number of oils and fats with butter and flour, onions and garlic, celery and bell pepper, to produce a rich base flavor

which will permeate the entire dish. "Nothing in Cajun country has a greater aroma than a light brown roux simmering with onions, celery, bell pepper and garlic" (John D. Folse, *The Evolution of Cajun and Creole Cuisine*, Donaldson, Louisiana, 1990, p. 16). I am using "roux" in its developed Cajun sense, as the basic flavor which permeates everything.

65. See John 7:38.

66. See Matthew 16:26.

67. See 1 Corinthians 13.

68. See C.S. Lewis, *The Great Divorce* (New York, Collier Books: Macmillan Publishing Company, 1946).

69. See Athanasius, "On the Incarnation of the Word" §6 in *St. Athanasius: Select Works and Letters, Vol. IV* of *The Nicene and Post Nicene Fathers of the Christian Church,* second series, edited by Philip Schaff and Henry Wace (Grand Rapids: Eerdmans Publishing Company, reprint 1987).

70. "Thou hast made us for Thyself and our hearts are restless till they rest in Thee" (*The Confessions of St. Augustine,* translated by F. J. Sheed [London: Sheed and Ward, ninth impression, 1978], book I.i).

71. C.S. Lewis, as quoted in the movie, *The Shadowlands.*

72. Vladimir Lossky, *The Mystical Theology of the Eastern Church* (New York: St. Vladimir's University Press, 1998), p. 66.

73. Ronald Rolheiser, *The Holy Longing* (New York:Doubleday, 1999), p. 40.

74. See John 1:38.

Suggestions for Further Reading

Allchin, A. M. *Participation in God: A Forgotten Strand in Anglican Tradition.* London: Dartmon, Longman & Todd, 1988.

Anselm, *Cur Deus Homo.* Edinburgh: John Grant, 1909.

Appleyard, Bryan, *Understanding the Present,* Doubleday, 1992.

Athanasius, *On the Incarnation of the Word of God.* London: A. R. Mowbray & Comp., reprint, 1963.

— "Against the Arians." In *St. Athanasius: Select Works and Letters, Vol. IV* of *The Nicene and Post Nicene Fathers of the Christian Church,* second series, edited by Philip Schaff and Henry Wace. Grand Rapids: Eerdmans Publishing Company, reprint 1987.

Aulen, Gustaf, *Christus Victor.* London: SPCK, 1950.

Barth, Karl. *Church Dogmatics.* Edinburgh: T & T Clark.

— "The Miracle of Christmas." In *Church Dogmatics* 1/2, pp. 172-202.

— "The Problem of a Correct Doctrine of the Election of Grace." In *Church Dogmatics* 2/2, p. 3-93.

— "Faith in God the Creator." In *Church Dogmatics* III/1, pp. 3-41.

— "Creation as Benefit." In *Church Dogmatics* III/1, pp. 330-344.

— "God with Us." In *Church Dogmatics* IV/1, pp. 3-21.

— "The Covenant as the Presupposition of Reconciliation." In *Church Dogmatics* IV/1, pp. 22-54.

— "The Way of the Son of God into the Far Country." In *Church Dogmatics* IV/1, pp. 157-211.

— "The Judge Judged in our Place." In *Church Dogmatics* IV/1, pp. 211-283.

— "The Homecoming of the Son of Man." In *Church Dogmatics* IV/2, pp. 36-116.

— "The Sloth and Misery of Man." In *Church Dogmatics* IV/2, pp. 378-483.

Berry, Wendell. *What Are People For?* New York: North Point Press, 1990.

Bryson, Bill, *A Short History of Nearly Everything,* Doubleday, 2003.

Buckley, Michael J. *At the Origins of Modern Atheism.* New Haven: Yale University Press, 1987.

Buechner, Frederick. *Telling Secrets.* San Francisco: Harper, 1991.

Calvin, John. *The Institutes of the Christian Religion,* edited by John T. McNeill and translated by Ford Lewis Battles. Philadelphia: The Westminster Press.

Campbell, John McLeod. *The Nature of the Atonement.* Reprint with Introduction by James B. Torrance. Grand Rapids: Wm. B. Eerdmans Publishing Company, 1996.

Capon, Robert Farrar. *The Mystery of Christ and Why We Don't Get It.* Grand Rapids: Eerdmans Publishing Company, 1993.

Chesterton, G. K. *The Everlasting Man.* San Francisco: Ignatius Press, 1993.

Dorrien, Gary. *The Barthian Revolution in Modern Theology.* Louisville: Westminster John Knox Press, 2000.

Gunton, Colin. *The One, the Three and the Many.* Cambridge: Cambridge University Press, 1993.

— *The Triune Creator.* Grand Rapids: Eerdmans Publishing Company, 1998.

Eldredge, John and Brent Curtis *The Sacred Romance.* Nashville:Thomas Nelson Publishers, 1997.

Erskine, Thomas. *The Unconditional Freeness of the Gospel.* Edinburgh: Waugh and Innes, 1829.

Farrow, Douglas B. "The Doctrine of the Ascension in Irenaeus and Origen." The Journal of the Faculty of Religious Studies, McGill 26, (1998), pp. 31-50.

Ford, David F., Editor, *The Modern Theologians,* Blackwell Publishers, 1997.

Forsyth, P. T. *The Work of Christ.* London: Hodder and Stoughton, reprint 1946.

Friedman, Edwin H., *Friedman's Fables,* Guilford Press, 1990.

Hart, Trevor. *The Teaching Father: An Introduction to the Theology of Thomas Erskine of Linlathen.* Edinburgh: St. Andrews Press, The Devotional Library, 1993.

— *Faith Thinking.* London: SPCK 1995.

Hartwell, Herbert. *The Theology of Karl Barth: An Introduction.* London: Gerald Duckworth & Company, 1964.

Hawthorne, Gerald. *The Presence and the Power.* Dallas: Word Publishing, 1991.

Herrick, James A., *The Making of the New Spirituality,* InterVarsity Press, 2000.

Houston, James M. *In Pursuit of Happiness.* Colorado Springs: NavPress, 1996.

Howatch, Susan, *Glittering Images,* Ballantine Books, 1987.

Hunsinger, George. *How to Read Karl Barth.* New York: Oxford University Press, 1991.

Kruger, C. Baxter. *Parable of the Dancing God.* Jackson, Mississippi: Perichoresis Press, 1995.

— *God Is For Us.* Jackson, Mississippi: Perichoresis Press, 1995.

— *Home.* Jackson, Mississippi: Perichoresis Press, 1996.

— *The Secret.* Jackson, Mississippi: Perichoresis Press, 1997.

Lewis, C. S. "The Weight of Glory," in *The Weight of Glory and Other Essays.* Grand Rapids: Eerdmans Publishing Company, 1965, pp. 1-15.

— "Beyond Personality: Or First Steps in the Doctrine of the Trinity." In *Mere Christianity.* New York: Collier Books, Macmillan Publishing Company, 1960, pp. 135-190.

— *The Great Divorce.* New York: Collier Books, Macmillan Publishing Company, 1946.

— *Till We Have Faces.* New York: A Harvest Book, Harcourt Brace Jovanovich, Publishers, 1980.

— *The Chronicles of Narnia.* New York: Collier Books, Macmillan Publishing Company, 1946.

— *Surprised By Joy.* New York: A Harvest Book, Harcourt Brace and Company, 1984.

Loder, James E. and W. Jim Neidhardt, *The Knights Move: The Relational Logic of the Spirit in Theology and Science.* Colorado Springs: Helmers & Howard, 1992.

MacDonald, George. *The Golden Key.* Grand Rapids: Eerdmans Publishing Company, reprint 1982.

— *The Fisherman's Lady,* edited by Michael R. Phillips. Minneapolis: Bethany House Publishers, 1982.

— *The Marquis' Secret,* edited by Michael R. Phillips. Minneapolis: Bethany House Publishers, 1982.

McGrath, Alister E. *Iustitia Dei: A History of the Christian Doctrine of Justification.* Cambridge: Cambridge University Press, second edition, 1998.

Migliore, Daniel. "The Triune God" and "The Good Creation" in *Faith Seeking Understanding.* Grand Rapids: Eerdmans Publishing Company, 1991.

Miller, J. Keith. *The Secret Life of the Soul*. Nashville: Broadman and Holman Publishers, 1987.

Murphy, Michael. *Golf in the Kingdom*. New York: Penguin Books, 1992.

Niesel, Wilhelm. *The Theology of Calvin*. London: Luttwerworth Press, 1956.

Phillips, Michael R. *George MacDonald: Scotland's Beloved Storyteller*. Minneapolis: Bethany House, 1987.

Placher, William C. *The Domestication of Transcendence*. Louisville, Westminster: John Knox Press, 1996.

Richard of St. Victor, "Book Three of the Trinity" in *Richard of St. Victor*. New York: Paulist Press, 1979.

Smail, Thomas. *The Forgotten Father*. London: Hodder and Stoughton, 1987.

Tarnas, Richard. *The Passion of the Western Mind*. New York: Ballantine Books, 1993.

Taylor, John V. *The Go-Between God*. London: SCM Press, 1982.

Torrance, T. F. *The Mediation of Christ*. Grand Rapids: Eerdmans, 1983.

— *Preaching Christ Today*. Grand Rapids: Eerdmans, 1994.

— *The Trinitarian Faith: The Evangelical Theology of the Ancient Catholic Church*. Edinburgh: T & T Clark, 1988.

— "The Atoning Obedience of Christ." Moravian Theological Seminary Bulletin (1959) pp. 65-81.

— "The Resurrection and the Person of Christ" and "The Resurrection and the Atoning Work of Christ." In *Space, Time and Resurrection*. Edinburgh: The Handsel Press, 1976, pp. 46-84.

— "The Eclipse of God" and "Cheap and Costly Grace." In *God and Rationality*. London: Oxford University Press, 1971, pp. 29-85.

— "Karl Barth and the Latin Heresy." In *Karl Barth: Biblical and Evangelical Theologian*. Edinburgh: T & T Clark, 1990, pp. 213-240.

Torrance, J. B. *Worship, Community and the Triune God of Grace*. Downers Grove: IVP, 1996.

— "Covenant or Contract." Scottish Journal of Theology 23 #1 (Feb 1970).

— "The Vicarious Humanity of Christ." In *The Incarnation: Ecumenical Studies in the Nicene-Constantinopolitan Creed*, edited by T. F. Torrance, pp. 127-147. Edinburgh: The Handsel Press, 1981.

von Balthasar, Hans Urs. "Our Capacity for Contemplation" in *Prayer*. New York: Sheed & Ward. pp. 27-67.

Ware, Kallistos. "The Human Person as an Icon of the Trinity." Sobernost, vol. 8 # (1986) pp. 6-23.

— *The Orthodox Way.* London: Mowbray, 1979.

Webster, John. *Barth's Ethics of Reconciliation.* Cambridge: Cambridge University Press, 1995.

Weinandy, Thomas G. *In the Likeness of Sinful Flesh.* Edinburgh: T & T Clark, 1993.

Wink, Walter, *Naming the Powers,* Fortress Press, 1984

Wink, Walter, *Unmasking the Powers,* Fortress Press, 1986

9 781573 833455